The Battle of Base-Ball

THE MCFARLAND HISTORICAL BASEBALL LIBRARY

1. Cobb, Ty. *Busting 'Em and Other Big League Stories* (1914). 2003

2. Axelson, G.W. *"Commy": The Life Story of Charles A. Comiskey* (1919). 2003

3. Ellard, Harry. *Base Ball in Cincinnati: A History* (1907). 2004

4. Richter, Francis C. *Richter's History and Records of Base Ball, the American Nation's Chief Sport* (1914). 2005

5. Lanigan, Ernest J. *Baseball Cyclopedia* (1922). 2005

6. Evers, John J., and Hugh S. Fullerton. *Touching Second* (1910). 2005

7. Rice, Grantland. *Base-Ball Ballads* (1910). 2005

8. Claudy, C.H. *The Battle of Base-Ball* (1912). 2005

9. Kelly, Mike "King." *"Play Ball": Stories from the Diamond Field and Other Historical Writings about the 19th Century Hall of Famer* (1888). 2006.

10. Anonymous and Noah Brooks. *The Great Match* [1877] *and Our Base Ball Club* [1884]*: Two Novels from the Early Days of Base Ball*, volume editors Trey Strecker *and* Geri Strecker. 2010

11. Green, Guy W. *The Nebraska Indians* [1900] *and Fun and Frolic with an Indian Ball Team* [1907]*: Two Accounts of Baseball Barnstorming at the Turn of the Twentieth Century*, volume editor Jeffrey P. Beck. 2010

12. Salsinger, H.G. *Ty Cobb: Two Biographies—"Our Ty: Ty Cobb's Life Story" (1924) and "Which Was Greatest: Ty Cobb or Babe Ruth?" (1951)*, volume editor William R. Cobb. 2012

13. Joss, Addie. *Addie Joss on Baseball: Collected Newspaper Columns and World Series Reports, 1907–1909*, compiled and annotated by Rich Blevins. 2012

The Battle of Base-Ball

by C. H. Claudy

Including
"How I Became a Big-League Pitcher"
by Christy Mathewson

McFarland Historical Baseball Library, 8
Gary Mitchem *and* Mark Durr, *Editors*

McFarland & Company, Inc., Publishers
Jefferson, North Carolina, and London

Frontispiece: Christy Mathewson, famous pitcher of the New York National League Club.

Library of Congress Cataloguing-in-Publication Data

Claudy, C. H. (Carl Harry), 1879–1957.
The battle of base-ball / by C. H. Claudy ; including "How I became a big-league pitcher" by Christy Mathewson.
[Gary Mitchem and Mark Durr, series editors]
p. cm. — (McFarland historical baseball library ; 8)
[Originally published: New York : The Century Co., 1912. With new editors' note.]
Includes index.

ISBN 0-7864-2020-0 (softcover : 50# alkaline paper) ♾

1. Baseball—United States—Juvenile literature. 2. Baseball—Rules—Juvenile literature. I. Title: Battle of baseball. II. Mathewson, Christy, 1880–1925. III. Title. IV. Series.
GV863.A1C53 2005
796.357—dc22 2005004861

British Library cataloguing data are available

On the cover: The 1910 and 1911 world champion Philadelphia Athletics at Shibe Park

Manufactured in the United States of America

McFarland & Company, Inc., Publishers
Box 611, Jefferson, North Carolina 28640
www.mcfarlandpub.com

To
All American Boys in General

And to
Carl Harry Claudy, Jr.
In Particular

Acknowledgments

Material for "The Battle of Base-ball" has been gathered from many sources, and many different authorities have contributed opinions and suggestions that have been of great assistance. The book is especially indebted to the interesting incidents and explanations found in the base-ball writings of Mr. Hugh S. Fullerton; to the illuminating points set forth in the clever base-ball comment of Mr. J. E. Grillo in the Washington *Star*; and to the courtesy of Mr. J. C. Morse, Editor of *The Baseball Magazine*, in placing at the author's disposal a complete file of that authoritative and entertaining periodical; and to Mr. James E. Sullivan of the American Sports Publishing Company, for kind permission to reprint the Simplified Rules of Base-ball by Mr. A. G. Spalding.

The information and advice herein set forth are furthermore enriched by the able and interesting chapter by the well-known pitcher of the New York Giants, Christy Mathewson—"How I Became a Big-League Pitcher."

Last, but by no means least, the author wishes to offer his grateful acknowledgments to his friend, Robert H. Young, son of that "Uncle Nick" Young, whose name is beloved by base-ball players and base-ball lovers alike. Mr. Young has kindly given the entire manuscript a careful reading, and, from his deep knowledge of the game, has contributed many suggestions and keen criticisms of the greatest value.

To all of these, and to the many professional players whose memories and experience have been drawn upon for story, incident or advice, the author's sincere thanks are due, and are most heartily tendered.

THE AUTHOR.

Contents

Contents

List of Illustrations

List of Illustrations

Editors' Note

During the last decades of the nineteenth century and the first of the twentieth, hundreds of instructional baseball books and articles were written and marketed, primarily to adolescents. Attributed to the likes of Henry Chadwick, Tim Murnane, Johnny Evers, Christy Mathewson, and Nap Lajoie, as well as a number of less prominent names from both inside and outside the game, the baseball how-to helped satisfy the appetite for outdoor recreation that an industrialized America had recently awakened to. With televised baseball still years away and the major leagues concentrated in the East, many Americans interested in playing baseball relied on written descriptions of their favorite players' techniques and strategies. These were found occasionally in detailed game accounts and, more often, in books and periodicals such as Chadwick's *Base Ball: How to Learn It, How to Play It and How to Teach It*, Spalding's Athletic Library series and *Baseball Magazine*.

Carl H. Claudy's *Battle of Base-Ball* has much in common with the many other instructional books of its day—chapters on each of the facets of the game, a contribution from a star player, photographs of big leaguers in action, anecdotes—but differs in one notable way. The book turns on an extended metaphor—baseball as war.

Editors' Note

The description of baseball in terms of battle and weaponry was hardly new. Baseball had from its earliest days employed such language. At least as early as 1868, the pitcher was called "the battery" (by 1897 the term was extended to include the catcher); by 1905, he was said to have been "bombed" if he gave up many hits in an inning or a game; and by 1910, he was known as the "artillerist." In 1881, a "rifle shot" was a hard throw; by 1890, it was a line drive. After World War I the term "casualty pass" was used to describe a base on balls, and after the Second World War, walked batsmen were said to be given their "furlough." Over the years many more expressions have rounded out baseball's vocabulary of violence: fielders "gun down" runners and turn "twin killings"; pitchers aim "cannon shots" and "fireballs" at hitters who blast "screaming meemies" at the defense and "bombs" out of the park.

Even for those aware of the relationship between baseball and war implicit in the sport's terminology, Claudy's metaphor strikes an odd note in a book for young readers. There is discussion of players' proper "subjection to discipline"; the likening of rules prohibiting "certain kinds of balls, shoes, gloves" to the outlawing of "expanding or mushroom bullets, or poisoned swords or bayonets"; a passing mention of "crippl[ing] the enemy"—though in a passage in which Claudy outlines differences between war and sport—and even a chapter title that seems to pun on the word "Arms," all of which will raise a few eyebrows today. Mixed in with these discussions are the repeated encouragements toward honor, hard work, and fair play that demonstrate Claudy's awareness of a formative young audience. His term "civilized warfare" suggests the apparent twin motives of the book, pointing to both the ideal of American masculinity it endorses ("all boys," the author writes, "like their American fathers, like a good fight, a fair fight, a square fight") and a countervailing emphasis on self-restraint and the cultivation of conscience presumably aimed at an audience of willful young men. The book would be worth reading just to see how and in how many ways Claudy handles the two themes. Consider the challenge of adapting his baseball-war comparison to a number of instructional chapters on offense and defense—something Claudy is equal to—and the book makes for irresistible reading.

The Battle of Base-Ball wasn't Claudy's first published work for adolescents. He was an accomplished writer for this audience, having published a number of primers and juvenile novels and contributed to magazines such as *St. Nicholas* and *American Boy. The Battle of Base-Ball* was, however, his only book-length publication on the national pastime; as a freelance writer and a correspondent for the *New York Herald*, he wrote on a wide range of other topics and had a number of interests. He was long active within the Freemasons, steadily publishing articles and books about the society, and was a noted photographer with an interest in aviation. (Claudy was a friend of the Wright brothers, and his photographs of their early flights are today at the Smithsonian.) By the time he died, on May 27, 1957, he had amassed a body of work that included some 32 books and more than 1,600 essays, articles, short stories, and poems.

Virtually all of his published writing on baseball came in the three-year period leading up to and just following the 1912 publication of his book. Some of the chapters—batting, running, offensive game planning, the pitcher-catcher battery, fielding, and defensive strategy—appeared in an early form as a series of seven instructional and anecdotal articles in consecutive issues of *St. Nicholas* in 1911. The articles would stand as chapters in the book, along with a handful of other pieces Claudy wrote to supplement them, and this main text was joined to celebrity articles by Christy Mathewson and and A.G. Spalding. Mathewson, whose *Pitching in a Pinch* was brought out in 1912, originally published "How I Became a Big-League

Pitcher" that same year, in the June Issue of *St. Nicholas*. Al Spalding's "Simplified Rules" appeared annually in *The Spalding Guides* beginning with the 1910 issue.

The McFarland edition of C.H. Claudy's *Battle of Base-Ball* exactly reproduces the text of the original, including any peculiarities of spelling and punctuation, and any historical inaccuracies. While the acknowledgments in the original edition seem to indicate that Claudy preferred a lowercase *b* after the hyphen in *Base-ball*, the use of capital letters for both *B*s on the title and half-title pages and an inconsistency in the rendering of the word in the text left room for doubt. (The term appears first with and then without its hyphen, for instance, in the titles atop Chapter I.) The editors have chosen to capitalize both elements in *Base-Ball* for the title but to preserve any variant forms in the text. The pagination of this edition has been adjusted to fit series specifications, and some photographs have been re-sized, their placement in most instances minimally affected. An index and this note have been added. The photograph on the cover of the McFarland edition was chosen by the editors; it also appears in chapter X, as in the original.

The editors gratefully acknowledge editor and English professor Trey Strecker, who early suggested *The Battle of Base-Ball* as a prospect for the McFarland Historical Baseball Library, and later volunteered to compile an index for the book; the SABR Bibliography Committee, especially Andy McCue; Joanne Kemp, adult services librarian of the Ashe County (N.C.) Library, and Pam Mitchem, instructor and assistant archivist at Appalachian State University, who provided source and research material in the production of this edition.

Mark Durr
Gary Mitchem

Preface

Base-ball, the great American game, occupies a unique position among sports. It has a greater patronage than any other sport can boast, anywhere in the world. It has so large an attendance that base-ball statisticians have given up trying to get and collate the figures, realizing the impossibility of accuracy! In 1910, 7,256,525 people saw the big league games—in 1911, no one knows how many, but it was unquestionably a much larger number. Then, of course, there were, besides, countless thousands who watched the minor league games, and almost the entire male population of the country must have seen some amateur games!

No other game has professional players of such high personal standing as the modern professional ball-players (of whom, in the big league clubs, more than fifty are college graduates), or pays its players any such sums as are paid to American base-ball players, whose salaries frequently run into the thousands of dollars a year (and, in two instances at least, to the sum of ten thousand dollars a year).

No other game of any kind makes so universal an appeal in America. At any league park, on any playing day of the year, one can see a newsboy, a bank president, a laborer, a society man, a streetcar conductor, and a judge sitting side by side enjoying the same sport, with an equal full understanding of its complicated rules and plays.

No other sport can boast of so much intense excitement with so little personal danger. The only other games at all comparable with it in intensity of action and excitement, foot-ball, hockey, polo, etc., are all dangerous to limb and sometimes to life. Base-ball, while by no means without occasional danger, seldom records a fatality.

Base-ball, playable only in fair and warm weather, works harm to neither player nor spectator. Cold weather base-ball is out of the question, for the simple reason that players cannot handle the ball with cold fingers. If it could be played during the winter, undoubtedly many people would get severe colds, if nothing worse, from watching it, and many players severe injuries from playing and sliding on frozen ground. As it is, these things do not happen.

Base-ball combines quickness of action, quickness of thought, intense bodily activity, and generalship and strategy, without making extreme demands upon physical strength. Small and light men make good ball-players, as well as large and heavy ones. But all, naturally strong or with but moderate muscular development, must be trained to the second in quickness of action, and must keep in perfect physical trim if the game is to be played at its best; and so high a standard has been won in the skill of major league players that the public will not tolerate in its favorite sport anything but the best of play.

During the playing season, every newspaper in the great cities devotes columns to the sport; some of them whole pages. Special editors and writers are employed to "cover" the base-ball assignments. And because of this interest taken in the game by those who want to read of it as well as see it, a special base-ball language has grown up, a language which is partly slang and partly technical terms of the game, as intelligible to the base-ball "fan" (short for fanatic) as it is meaningless to those who do not love the sport, and so, learn its pithy jargon.

It is, therefore, the author's hope that this book will not be too severely criticized from a literary standpoint if some echoes of this special language creep into the text, since to report matters concerning the game without departing sometimes from the language held as a model in schools is almost impossible.

There have been so many books written on base-ball from so many different angles, that to show it from any side not a familiar one is well nigh impossible. Yet too many of the stories of the game as written for the younger player either consider him as absolutely ignorant of its principles and so antagonize that lad who probably knows the rules of the game better than his instructor, or else are written so technically and for players of such mature age, that boys look in vain for that helpfulness which may fit their own especial needs.

As no one man knows all of base-ball, so no one book can tell all its mighty story. But an earnest attempt has been made here to get at the heart of the game and tell of it from a boy's standpoint, and to show him, not only the wonders done by skilled players and fine teams, but how he, too, can become skillful, and, in part at least, do for himself, and for his team, what his favorite base-ball idol does frequently in a game of the major or minor leagues.

Base-ball has many points in common with warfare, albeit different enough in purpose and methods. As explained in the first chapter, these points of similarity are actual, not imagined; in making the comparison, no stretching of a point for the sake of a pleasing imagery has been attempted.

Preface

And on these lines, believing that all boys, like their American fathers, like a good fight, a fair fight, a square fight, without favor and with "May the best man win" for a sentiment, this book is written.

C. H. Claudy.
Washington, D.C.,
February 1, 1912.

THE BATTLE OF BASE BALL

Chapter I

Base-ball a Battle of Brains as Well as Skill

"Battle? I thought it was a *game*!" some mother or sister may say, after reading the title, and before the season has educated them.

But, when you come to think of it, base-ball is a battle. It has its generals, its captains, its lieutenants, its rank and file. It has its grand strategy, its tactics, and its drill. It has its battlefield, its arms, and its equipment. It is a battle with rules, to be sure, but then, a real battle, between real armies, is also fought according to certain rules, called by nations the laws of civilized warfare. These rules prohibit, for instance, the use of expanding or mushroom bullets, or poisoned swords or bayonets. The rules of the battle of base-ball prohibit certain kinds of balls, shoes, gloves. Civilized warfare recognizes the flag of truce, and will not permit a man carrying one to be shot. He is safe so long as he has the white flag. Base-ball, in which the end and aim of the defense is to put a man "out," permits a soldier of the enemy to be safe from danger of being "put out" so long as he keeps his foot upon any of the white bags used as bases. Drill and discipline are the backbone at once of the company and the army-corps. History gives many instances in which a numerically superior force

McGraw,
Manager of the New York Giants
Popularly known as "The Little Napoleon of Baseball"

has been routed by a much smaller but well-trained body of soldiers. In base-ball, the preliminary training, drill, and subjection to discipline mean everything when it comes to winning games—battles. In war the individually brilliant and brave man frequently performs some remarkable act, and lives forever as a hero, as Pickett at Gettysburg, or Hobson at Santiago Harbor; but it is the men who think first of the good of the entire army, and the success of the campaign, who win the battles.

Tyrus Cobb, the star batsman of the Detroit team, American League, may steal home in a world series, or Neal Ball, of Cleveland, make an unassisted triple play and get a gold medal for it, or Frank Baker make two home runs in a world's series and all but win it single handed; but in the long run the greater credit should be given the men who play for the team and the game, and not their own records, in base-ball, as well as in warfare.

There are just two sides to a battle—offense and defense. There are just two parts to a base-ball game—offense and defense. In a battle the offense concerns itself with capturing a station, a city, occupying a position, driving the enemy before it. The main idea in modern warfare is not, "How many men can we kill?" but, "How much can we win from the enemy?" In base-ball, the offense strives to occupy certain stations (bases) and win a certain city (home). The attempt is made to do this in the best, the quickest, the easiest way, and not at all necessarily by "killing" the greatest number of pitched balls. The man who stands at the plate and patiently "waits out" a pitcher for a base on balls, with the bases full, is doing just as much to win a victory for his team as he who stands at the plate and bats the ball far out beyond the enemy's reach.

In warfare a general entering a campaign will plan it with every care. He will lay out his battles as exactly as he can, decide which troops he will use in different situations, what tricks he will employ to fool the enemy and discount, as far as possible, the enemy's offense, by a patient study of his resources, possibilities, and strength.

Long before the Philadelphia Athletics and the Chicago Cubs had won the championships in their respective leagues in 1910, "Connie Mack" and Frank Chance were gathering information, each about the other and the other's team. Mack knew, and saw that his pitchers knew, all that could be learned about each and every member of Chance's mighty machine—just what balls each man hit easiest, just which way the majority of their hits went, just what the average speed of each man on the team might be, just how far each might be allowed to take a "lead" from first without drawing a useless throw from the pitcher, just what their tactics would be in any one of a dozen situations.

And Chance, you may be sure, was learning all he could of the weaknesses and the strength of the Athletics—which men might be easily "rattled," which men must be played for on their merits, just what to do with each of Mack's staff of wonderful pitchers, just what kind of a game would be most apt to beat him.

In 1911 there were several interviews printed in many newspapers in which it was vehemently denied that either Connie Mack of

Cornelius McGillicuddy
Popularly known as "Connie Mack," Manager of the Philadelphia Athletics

the Philadelphia Athletics or McGraw of the New York Giants (pennant winners in the two major leagues), had any interest in seeing their opponents-to-be, in a game. They would win by "straight" base-ball, these two; they were up to no tricks, these recognized foxes of base-ball warfare; they would employ no scouts to watch the enemy! Yet the expert at the game could note that no pitcher or catcher was in doubt as to what kind of a ball should be pitched any batsman, and the small number of stolen bases shows the knowledge pitchers had of the amount of "lead" each and every base runner could be permitted. It was deemed necessary for the good of the coming games, to deny any plan-laying in advance, but it is a pretty safe conclusion that if there was anything McGraw didn't know about the Athletics or Mack about the Giants it was because neither was able to get more information, not that neither tried.

In defense an army endeavors to cripple the enemy, to prevent him carrying out his designs, to bother and annoy him wherever possible, to render his strategy useless and his plans of no effect. In base-ball the entire end and aim of the defense is to make the third "out" as quickly as possible, to do it, if it can be done, without allowing a man of the offense to occupy even the first station on the road to the city they would capture.

"To make the third out as quickly as possible" is usually true. Once in a while there will be a purposeful delay. If it is possible to get a pitcher caught between bases and to "run him down" it is an old, old base-ball trick to "let him live" as long as he is willing to dodge up and down the path in the hope finally of evading his opponents, because a tired and winded pitcher is not able to pitch so fast a ball, nor with such good control, as is he who refuses to "bite" on any such trick and who, seeing he must eventually be retired submits gracefully to the inevitable and allows himself to be touched out. In an amateur game played in Washington, D. C., in 1911, a pitcher was "whip-sawed" in a much more clever style than by being run down between bases, by a trick which would fool no league player but which did fool this particular pitcher to the limit. He got on first base by an error, a genuine, dyed-in-the-wool, accidental error, an overthrow of first by the short stop. The score was tied, there were two out and the eighth inning, and of course, the runner kept on for second. The first baseman, recovering the ball, threw to second. The center-fielder was backing up the second baseman. The second baseman deliberately let the ball through his hands, and the runner, now certain of doing something for his team, kept on to third, where the center-fielder easily retired him, by a neat throw to the third baseman, who almost dropped the ball from laughing at the trick. For that made the third out, the now panting runner had to go immediately to the pitcher's box, and before the ninth inning was over, he had been found for five singles, which, with an error, netted four runs, winning the game.

An army has nerves, even as has the human body. When you want to throw a ball, your brain sends a message to the muscles of your arm to do thus-and-so, and the arm does it. When the brain of an army, its commanding general, wants to order an attack or retreat, he sends a message, by means of the army's nerves—wires, telegraph instruments, wireless instruments, signal flags, signal lanterns, etc., manipulated by his Signal Corps, and the branch or arm signaled to, responds.

Just as the nerves of an army are its signals, so the nerves of a base-ball team are the signals or signs by which the captain or manager directs the play, and by which players inform each other what is about to be done. Neglect them, and the members of the team play each one for himself. Imagine a battle in which each regiment attempted to do just what it thought best to do, opposed to an army which was under the direction of one master brain!

Interrupting an army's signals, stealing its intelligence by making a secret connection with its telegraph-wires, capturing its messengers and reading its despatches, has always been one of the romances of war. And reading the signals of an opposing team, learning what they are going to do before they do it, and frustrating their attempt, is a favorite strategy in base-ball. But, just as it is against the law of nations to shoot with a mushroom bullet, which is needlessly cruel, even if certain, so it is against the laws of fair play, which distinguishes college ball and school ball and all boyhood "fair-play" ball, to steal signals of an opposing team except upon the field, and by any other method than that of observation, acute watchfulness, and clever knowledge of play. It is said that the Chicago "White Sox," in one game in which they thought their signals were being read, changed signals entirely, not once or twice, but at every inning—nine times in a nine-inning game! It meant work beforehand to learn nine sets of signals, but it assured the men that their opponents were not getting their pitcher's intentions before he had delivered the ball!

On the other hand, it is claimed that Eddie Collins, that wonderful scintillating star of second baseman, of the now twice World's Champion Philadelphia Athletics, was able to guess the signals of the National League Champion club—the Chicago "Cubs"—in the 1910 World Series, and, by no other means than his eyes and his cleverness, warn his team-mates what to expect on the field. If so, it was a splendid exhibition of base-ball strategy, a part of the game, entirely honest and wholly creditable. Little Johnny Evers, the Chicago second baseman, the man who has been the center about which the entire Chicago team revolved for several years, is credited with being not only a lightning thinker, but a very acute observer, and able to guess plays, call the ball which is coming, and frustrate tricks of the opposing team with quite uncanny skill.

When catcher Schmidt was with Detroit he gave signals to his pitchers with his hands, as do most catchers, but he also used his eyes, particularly when runners were on bases. This double system gave him a chance to signal two things at once, one for his own team, the other for a possible guesser. But sometimes the possible guesser outguesses the man who would fool him! In the games between Pittsburgh and Detroit for the World's Championship, 1909, Tommy Leach, the center-fielder of the "Pirates," had the happy thought that if Schmidt said one thing with his hands, he was saying another with his eyes. Close observation verified this, and so it frequently happened that the Pittsburgh batsmen knew, just as well as Schmidt, what his signals were. This was legitimate signal stealing, just as the capture and use of the enemy's telegraph-line, or the detection of his wireless message, is a legitimate strategy in warfare.

There was some talk, following the 1911 World's Series, that the Philadelphia team was able to get so many hits off Marquard and Mathewson because they had detected the battery's signals. The method supposed to have been used, according to these stories, was this: Philadelphia has a "mascot," a little hunchback who dresses in a Philadelphia uniform, and sits with the players, collecting the bats and arranging them for the batters. Many patrons of the game will recall having seen him with a big catcher's mit, tossing and catching the ball with a pitcher before a game. According to these stories, this bat-boy would see the Giant's signals when he walked out to pick up the bat the batsman discarded. Being near the ground, on account of his small stature, he was supposed to be able to see under the catcher's bent knee. Learning the signal, he would transmit it by signs to the coacher on third, who would inform the batsman what variety of pitched ball was coming.

Roger Bresnahan
The popular Catcher and Manager of the St. Louis Club, National League

There seems to be an element of far-fetched-ness in this attempt to account for the hitting done by the Philadelphia players. It is generally thought that "Matty" pitches his own games—that is, decides for himself what he will give the batter, instead of taking signals from his catcher, yet it was "Matty," the Great, who had to admit that, do what he would, he could not fool all the Philadelphia players, all the time.

It is not always the cool, cautious, calculating general who wins the battle. Sometimes the desperate, daring undertaking, the nervy willingness to risk all for a great gain, wins a great victory.

So it is in base-ball. The cool general, the calculating plan, wins often—but sometimes a desperate situation needs a desperate remedy. The base-ball general who can rise to the occasion is, then, the man to have at the head of a team.

When the Detroit club was fighting for every game in 1909—needed almost every game to win—there was a certain contest with the New York club, the "Yankees" or "Highlanders," in which Detroit was one run behind in the ninth inning. The batting order had rolled around in Manager Hugh Jenning's favor, and Owen Bush, the Detroits' midget short-stop, was up. He managed to draw a pass and rested on first. McIntyre, the next man who came to the bat, contrived to get hit by a pitched ball, and he took first, Bush, of course, getting second.

The cool, calculating general

Hugh Jennings
Manager of the American League Club "Detroits," popular called "The Tigers"

would have had Cobb, next up, "hit it out," in the hope that either he or Crawford would be able to bang in the tying run. But Jennings wanted two runs so badly he took no chance of "slugging" alone—slugging which might be fielded—bringing them in. He wanted a run to the good—not an extra inning tie. This was what he did: he put an extra "yah—yah" on his battle-cry, "Eeee—yah!" and then pulled up a few more sprigs of grass, and he was all the while instructing by signals his two runners and Cobb that a "delayed double steal" was the play. Cobb let the first ball go by. Bush did not take a great lead from second base, but McIntyre dashed for second. Kleinow, New York's back-stop, hurled the ball to second. McIntyre stopped midway, and Bush, with the catcher's throw, sprinted full-speed for third. La Porte, the New York second baseman, had no one on whom to make a play. Bush had fled, and McIntyre had not arrived! La Porte hesitated just a fraction of a second, then threw to Austin at third; but the fraction of a second was enough for little Bush, who slid in under Austin's leg—*safe*! Meanwhile, of course, McIntyre was on second. Then Cobb hit the next ball pitched for a single, *two* runs came in, the game was over, and Detroit had won!

It took nerve, daring, generalship, to try a delayed double steal at that moment, and, probably because of its very unexpectedness, it succeeded. No blame could be attached to the New York team, to Kleinow, La Porte, or Austin. They were merely, in that one instance, outguessed, out-played—outgeneraled! In some other game, no doubt, they turned the tables on the Detroits by some equally clever or timely play.

Warfare has its reserves. Many men went no nearer to a battlefield in the Spanish War than camp, but served no less because they did but "stand and wait." They were ready. They were in training. They were giving all their time and soul and energy to get ready to fight, march, capture, destroy, or protect, as their commanding officer

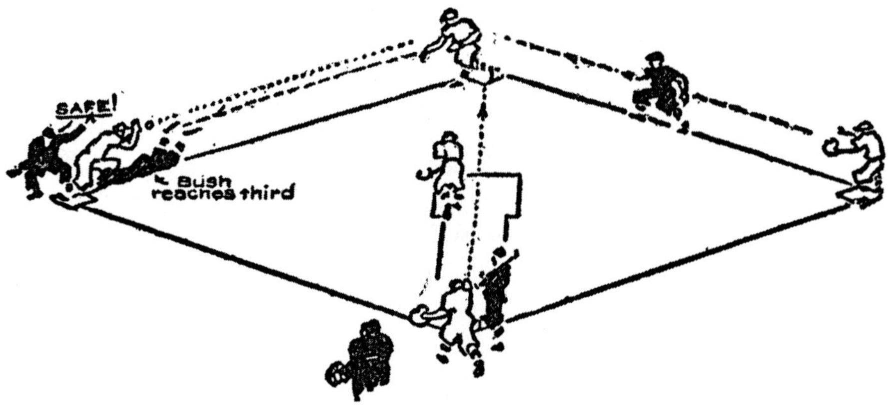

The delayed double steal. (See preceding page.)

might command. They had little enough of the glory, but an army without reserves would be fatally handicapped. So with a base-ball team. It has its reserves, its "second string," its substitutes. Many a big League team carries pitchers all season who seldom or never start a game—but there they are, pitching to the batters before the game for practice, working hard on the coaching lines, using their eyes, doing all they can to win for their team, though they may seldom toe the mound or run the paths. They must be ready to go in at any time, steady of nerve, confident in spite of the lack of confidence of their manager, which keeps them on the bench, able, in spite of lack of practice under fire, to do the work demanded of them.

Will any one say that "Topsy" Hartzell, for years center-fielder of the Athletics, but in 1911 not "holding down" a regular position on the team, did not deserve his full share of the World's Series prize money? Always in condition, always ready to jump into the game at a moment's notice, always able (or almost always) to deliver a hit when, as pinch-hitter, he was called on to save a game, he surely contributed no little to the success which crowned the efforts of his team—yet the greater part of the time he was among the "reserves" of that particular "base-ball army"—the most of the time he did but stand and wait.

Will any one say that "Dode" Criss, the celebrated "pinch-hitter" of the St. Louis Browns, would not have deserved his share of prize-money, had they been champions? A pitcher who seldom pitched, a man who seldom stepped to bat more than once in a game, he was known as the "champion pinch-hitter" of base-ball, the man most likely to make a hit when it was wanted, and who was put in at the fag-end of the game to relieve a pitcher who had done his work, in the often sustained hope that he would "hit it out." Notwithstanding that he spent most of his time upon the bench, all who know either warfare or base-ball will admit that he "also served" while he sat and patiently waited for his chance!

CHAPTER II

Batting

There are just two halves to the offense in a battle—getting there and fighting. The advantage is always with the side that gets there first and enjoys a secure position while the enemy is but getting into position to fight. Students of warfare and strategy will point to Napoleon as the great exampler of this—the general who believed in getting there *first*, if he was going to fight.

There are just two halves to base-ball offense—"getting on" and "getting home." Like Napoleon and his generalship, the lad who can so engineer his base-ball campaign as to enable one player of his side to get on and get home *first*, immediately places the opposing team in the position of having to fight an uphill game and of having to dislodge the enemy from his commanding position before beginning to win on their own account.

There are a number of ways to "get on" and a number of ways to "get home." But the principal way to get on is to hit the ball yourself, and the principal way to get home is to have several of your fellow-players hit it, and make what is called a "*safe* hit." So that batting is at least half, if not two-thirds, of the offense in base-ball.

The importance of good batters to a team can hardly be overestimated. It has been demonstrated that the finest defensive work, the cleverest "inside play," the most admirable generalship, are often ineffective before a team of "heavy hitters." The three most recent instances, as many of you remember, are the three championships won in succession by the Detroit "Tigers" in the American League, the fact that the Chicago "Cubs," considered the greatest "inside-ball" team ever put together, could not make even a good showing against a team like the Athletics, which insisted on pounding the ball far beyond the confines of the infield and all its defensive play, and, the overwhelming defeat administered to the New York Giants, pennant winners in the National League in 1911, by the Philadelphia Athletics, pennant winners in the American League.

Ask any fan who or what was responsible for the Athletics taking the World's Series and the reply will consist of a man's name—Baker. For while unquestionably the Athletics had, man for man, the better team, it is to Baker, Philadelphia's hard hitting third baseman, that they owe much of their victory.

Every World's Series has had its individual hero—more often than not, a most unexpected one. In 1903, when Pittsburgh and Boston fought it out, there was "Bill" Dineen, now an umpire, with a laurel wreath to wear after it was over. Christy Mathewson—the undefeatable "Big Six" who went down to honorable defeat in 1911, starred in 1905 in the inter-league series, in which the Giants bested the Athletics. George Rohe, in the memorable championship battles between the two Chicago teams, in 1906, had his name writ large in newspaper headlines; John Kling, great catcher and "Three Fingered" Brown, great pitcher, starred in the 1907 and 1908 battles between Chicago and Detroit; "Babe" Adams of Pittsburgh got into the limelight in no uncertain manner when Pittsburgh won out in the 1909 series with Detroit; and Eddie Collins, second baseman of the Philadelphia Athletics, by his hitting, fielding and great all-around playing, stood out preëminent among the Cub-Athletic players in the World's Series of 1910.

And in 1911 it was Frank Baker, third baseman of the Athletics, whose hitting broke up game after game and whose two historic home runs played havoc with the Giant's chances for the championship. It is his hitting which gets him special mention here and now, for Baker learned to bat by batting, and has not only batted himself to fame but his club to a championship. No fluke home runs, these, for Baker made many in the season just passed. Eleven times in 1911 he put the ball over the right field fence at Shibe Park in Philadelphia. Four other men have knocked balls over that fence—Baker has knocked fifteen altogether. But Baker did more than hit home runs in the inter-league series—he made several hits including a couple of two-baggers, and one of these, in the third game, earned him a tribute from the master

"Home-run" Baker
Who starred in the 1911 championship games

pitcher of the game, Mathewson, such as comes to but few players in a lifetime. For when Baker came to bat for the third time in the third game, Mathewson, sick of the hits Baker had been making off his delivery, passed him to first base amid a pandemonium of noise which was hardly exceeded by the victorious cheer ending the entire series—deliberately gave four balls, in open acknowledgment that here was a man so certain to make at least a base hit, that the greatest pitcher the game has at the present day, who owns one of the wisest heads in base-ball, believed it better to present him with the equivalent of a single than take chances of another double, triple or one of those base-clearing home runs!

It was a great triumph for the batting game, and it is worthy of note that, when Baker makes his long, low hits, which have such terrific driving power behind them that they often hit the fence if they don't go clean over it, he does not draw his bat 'round to the small of his back and take a mighty swipe at the ball! Instead he hits with a short, jerky, sharp chop, with the power of shoulders and forearms as well as wrists and body-swing in the ball. By this short, sharp stroke he is able to hit at and connect with a ball at or near its point of "breaking" (when the curve commences to show itself) and does not have to begin his swing long before the ball reaches him, as do sluggers who follow the plan of making mighty lunges at the ball in huge wide sweeps of the bat.

"Sluggers"—men who swing the bat far behind them and around again in a mighty sweep, hit with all their force at the place *where they believe the ball is going to be*. If it is somewhere else, they either fail to hit it, or pop up a fly, make a foul or perhaps hit it where they least expect it to go. Batters of the Baker type hit at the ball *where they know it is*, and consequently can the better gage what will happen to it after they hit it. The great "place hitters" have always been of the Baker type, hitting with short, sharp strokes of the bat. But, even so, place hitting is a rare faculty, as will be described later.

Baker is not the hardest hitter base-ball has ever known, he is by no means at the top of the list of men who are most certain to make a hit (Tyrus Cobb had an 1911 average of .420, which means that he made forty-two hits out of every one hundred opportunities to make a hit); but Baker is today one of the most feared men in base-ball, simply because he hits well with men on bases, hits hard and long and is never worried by crowds, talk, other players or over anxiety to hit the ball.

There are many kinds of good batters. There are men like Lajoie of Cleveland and Wagner of Pittsburgh, who hit anything and everything, and make both long hits and short hits. There are men like Cobb of Detroit, who are credited with an astonishing number of "singles"—not because they hit the ball so far, but because they get so quick a start and "beat it out" by speed alone. Cobb has often contended that his teammate Crawford was his superior with the bat, although, of course, Cobb holds the higher average. The Georgia boy says the difference is in his legs! There are men who hit better when hits are needed badly than at any other time, and who, like Dode Criss of the St. Louis "Browns," or Tinker of the "Cubs," while not particularly high in the batting averages, are of great value to their team when "at bat," because of this ability. There are men who hit "sacrifice flies" better than any other thing they do, men who "bunt" to perfection, and still others who, though not counted great batters, can almost always hit the delivery of certain pitchers. And there are occasionally men like Ed Delehanty, the greatest batsman who has yet played the game, who hit anything and everything all the time. Delehanty once made four home runs and a single in five times "at bat" in one game, a record which bids fair to stand forever!

All these various kinds of batters have their place on the team.

The arrangement of the batting order is an important part of a manager's or captain's work. Boys who organize a nine should follow the lead of the managers in the big Leagues, and arrange the batting order solely and entirely for the sake of getting the greatest number of runs. The first man up should be a good "waiter," a good hitter, a very fast man, and a very "heady" man. When Chicago played Philadelphia for the World's Championship, Sheckard of the Chicago "Cubs" led for his team, followed by Schulte, then Hofman, and then Chance. The Athletics put Strunk first, had Lord follow him, then came Collins, and then Baker.

The idea, of course, is that the first two men will, one or the other, or both, "get on" first base some way! Then will come two men who will either hit the ball hard and thus bring the runners round the diamond, or play the "hit and run" in order to make a score. But, be it noted, it frequently happens that the first man gets on, and—with no score, or a tied score or a one-run lead, or when one run behind and the game not too far advanced—the correct play is to make a "sacrifice" hit; hence, batter No. 2 should be a clever "bunter." During a part of the season of 1910, Killifer came after Milan in the Washington line-up, and in one game distinguished himself by making five perfect sacrifice bunts in five times up, every time advancing Milan to second, although getting thrown out himself!

Of course the batting order will not always "come right," but it will usually be at its best three times in a game, hence its arrangement is of the greatest importance. Note well that while the pitcher almost invariably is at the bottom of the list in a League team, he must not necessarily be so in a boy's team. If you have but one pitcher, play him where his batting ability warrants his being put, regardless of "big League" practice, which is occasioned by many circumstances that do not enter into a boy's game—one of them, for instance, being the great number of pitchers carried in the clubs of the major Leagues.

The way to learn to bat is to bat! There is no other way. But there are right and wrong ways of trying to bat. First of all, it is necessary to "stand to the plate." The player who gets three feet away and "reaches in" after balls is neither going to hit hard nor often. It is seldom that a batter is hit hard enough by a pitched ball to hurt him; if he is quick enough to bring his bat against the ball before it gets by, he should be quick enough to get out of the way of one which comes at him. Neither will it do to stand properly at the plate and yet "pull away" from it as the ball goes by. Even if you hit the ball, the very act of "pulling" will decrease the force of your blow, and if you are a right-hand hitter, "pulling" starts you

Ty Cobb
Universally admitted to be the greatest all-round ball-player the game has produced

away from first base instead of toward it. Left-hand hitters, too, must guard against "pulling away," since their eagerness to be off for first base often causes them to lean toward the base as the ball is delivered.

Pitchers soon discover this weakness, and put the ball on the extreme outside corner of the plate from the batter, with the result that he "fans" time after time. A sad example is found in the case of "Red" Walker, of Washington, a player who seemed a terror at the bat in the spring of 1911, but who developed the pulling habit so badly as almost entirely to destroy his value to his club.

Stand naturally, easily, with your feet together, if you can. Cobb and Lajoie—the American League batting leaders, the former champion with an average of .420, the latter ex-champion with a one-time average of .422—both stand easily, naturally, and swing with only moderate freedom at the ball.

"The great batters of our time," said Cobb, in and interview, "hold their bats a foot from the end, and, instead of swinging hard, aim to meet the ball flush. I like to 'swing,' but I can't afford to. So I stick to the sure system of meeting the ball 'fair' with a half-way grip on my bat."

Wagner of Pittsburgh, who is a terror to pitchers, stands with his feet more widely apart, and so do hosts of other good batters. Moreover, attempts to change the individual "style" of a batter are often fatal to his hitting; therefore, try to adopt a good style while you can, for if you get to standing awkwardly and play that way very often, an attempt to change may result in disaster to your average.

Whatever you do, don't try to use a bat which is too heavy for you. Perhaps there is no one thing that more retards a boy's game of ball, his development of skill, and his success as a player than his attempt to do everything the big League player does, merely *because* he does it, and without regard to the difference in age, strength, and size. (See Chapter VIII on "Drill, Battlefield and Arms.") There may be a boy on your team who has Cobb for his favorite; you see him buying a "Cobb" bat, long and slender, and trying to use it, although it is almost as big as he is! Some one who makes Anson, formerly of Chicago, or the "scrappy" little former New York player, "Kid" Elberfeld, his model, gets hold of a regular "war-club," thick, heavy, and short,—and finds he is hitting at the ball long after it has gone by! Choose your bat according to your size and strength; get one you can swing quickly, vigorously; and don't make the mistake of thinking a big club means lots of hits: it doesn't. If it did, every man playing would get the largest and heaviest bat he could carry. And hold it as seems natural to you, whether "choked" (that is, held some little way from the end) or right down on the end. Learn how you can hold the bat to make a bunt with the most certainty, and learn to take that hold instantly, and as the ball is pitched. To show the pitcher and the rest of the team that you are going to bunt by holding the bat as if for a bunt before the ball is pitched, is fatal to your success.

Learn to look at the pitcher all the time. This means while you are on the bench as well as when at the plate. A great part of the art of pitching consists in delivering all kinds of balls, fast, slow, curve, and straight, with, as nearly as possible, the same "motion." The better this can be done, the more effective the pitcher. But many pitchers, and particularly boys who have yet to learn all the art, have a different "motion" when pitching a curve from that which they use when pitching straight and fast. If you can learn this difference, you can the better judge, when at the plate, what is coming. Hence the advice to focus your eyes upon the opposing pitcher at all times.

Learn by constant practice to let the wide curve go by and to hit at the one that you think is going to be good; learn to judge the low ones and refuse to "bite" on those which are just teasingly near;

and don't be afraid of getting two strikes called on you. "It only takes one, you know," as the coachers say; a hit made from the seventh ball pitched is just as good as one made from the first. And don't be afraid of striking out. Players who fear or hate to be struck out are tempting bait for the pitcher's art; they get the reputation of hitting at everything after two strikes are called, and are often made to "pop up" fouls or hit easy grounders by having served to them a ball which the pitcher would never risk on a cool-headed batter who know how to wait for four balls.

Don't quarrel with the umpire because he calls "strike" when you let it go by because you thought it was going to be a "ball." He will make mistakes, because he is human. But it spoils the game to have any bickering—you know what happens in a big League game when some one disputes too vigorously the correctness of a called ball or strike!

And last, but not least, learn to "pull in" a swing at the ball. This is distinct from "pulling away." It is the art of starting a swing at a ball which "looks good," and curling the bat up in the arms when you see it is going to be bad, without making enough of a swing at it to make the umpire call a strike from your motion. Watch Chance, Crawford, Clarke, or "Red" Dooin, and see the artistic way in which they fail to hit even after they have started to! They have a "near strike" which is like the "near balk" of some pitchers—deceptive, but allowable!

Unless ordered to the contrary by the captain, your business, if there is no one on the bases, is to "get on." There are various ways. You can get to first base by "waiting out" the pitcher and getting four balls; by being "accidentally" hit with the ball; by an error in fielding, or by the catcher's drop of a third strike, and your "beating out the throw"; by making a hit which may and may not be so scored (a "scratch hit," as it is called); and, of course, by a clean base-hit.

You have no business to try to get on by deliberately allowing yourself to get hit with the ball. In the first place, it isn't, strictly speaking, fair. The rule permitting men to take first base when struck is designed to make the pitchers careful. It is not intended as a weapon of offense in the batter's hand. Jennings of the famous Baltimore Orioles (now manager for the Detroit team) used it as such a weapon of offense and did it so artistically and so often, that the rule was amended to its present form, whereby a batter must satisfy the umpire that he did not get hit on purpose, by making some obvious move to avoid the ball, before he can be allowed to take first because of being so struck. In the second place, it is dangerous, particularly to boys, who, naturally, have less skill in handling their bodies than grown men. So, if you are wise, you will not imitate those men in the big Leagues who have the reputation of being able to "get hit" so artistically that the umpire thinks they couldn't help it! Sometimes men overdo this in the big Leagues, in spite of the rule, and get the name of constantly trying to get hit, and so the umpires won't give them bases when they really are hit accidentally! Such a man was Ganley, of the Athletics, and things finally came to such a pass with him that, even when legitimately entitled to his base for being hit, he wouldn't move until the umpire ordered him to go!

It is needless to say that "getting on" is vital to scoring, for of course no one can score unless he reaches first base safely in some way. And with a player once there, his side's chances of scoring are enormously increased, not only by having the man on base to do the scoring, but by "tying up" fielders so that they can't work as effectively to put succeeding batsmen out. The first baseman, with no one on, plays for the batter. He gets where he thinks a hit will come, or where he can field it. And short-stop and second baseman play their positions to cover as much ground as possible.

Russell Ford
Of the New York Highlanders. A sensational pitcher

But, once let a man gain first base, and the baseman is held to the bag until the pitcher begins to "wind up," and either short-stop or second baseman must remain where he can reach second base to take a throw from the catcher, to stop a steal, or to receive a fielded ball to catch the man coming down from first. Consequently the second man at the bat has a much greater opportunity to make a hit than the first, provided No. 1 "gets on." It is for this reason, as well as others, that the first man up should be a "good waiter" and should be able to have two strikes and no balls called on him without getting nervous about letting a couple of "bad ones" go by.

And it is for this reason, too, that the first man should be a fast runner, since he will make first often on a slight error, such as a juggle or "boot" of the ball, where a slower man would fail. And never, never, never fail to "run it out," no matter how hopeless the chance may seem! Nine times out of ten, a fielded ball may beat you to the base; but the tenth time some one makes an error, and—you may score. There was a striking example of this recently in a game between the Detroits and the Washingtons in the American League. Washington was one run behind, the sixth inning, and at bat. There was a storm coming, one of those sudden, heavy thunderstorms that make a baseball field a lake within five minutes. Detroit was "stalling" for time and Washington playing its fastest. Washington tied the score, getting two men out and a man on third in the process; Detroit was raving, and Jennings, their manager, doing war-dances in the coacher's box.

Hal Chase
Premier first baseman of the game. Note that he is left-handed

The man at bat for Washington had the crowd with him—it was a big crowd, too. And he hit the ball! He hit it straight at little Owen Bush, who, ordinarily, is one of the best and most accurate short-stops of the League. Washington's batter felt that he was "out," to a certainty—that there wasn't a chance for him to get to first. The man on third trotted home, just as a formality, since the third "out" at first would make his crossing the plate of no avail. But the Washington batter "ran out" his hit. He ran hard, too, as if he meant it. And Bush, with plenty of time for the throw, nervously threw the ball five feet above the first baseman's extended hand,—whereupon the Washington runner danced on the base and waved his cap, the man on third trotted "home" with the winning run, the crowd went wild, and the next batter got himself put out in the shortest possible order. And then the rain came down in torrents and deluges, and there was no more playing that afternoon! But that one wild throw gave the game to Washington.

Had the batter failed to run out his hit, had he turned half-way down the path and walked to the bench—well, he didn't! And don't you, either; "run them out," no matter how hopeless the prospect seems. In the big Leagues they fine men who *don't* run them out, and if the managers think it's worth that much attention, be sure there is good reason back of it!

Don't bother with trying to learn "place hitting" or "batting to the opening."

"Hit 'em where he ain't," said McGraw to Bridwell of the "Giants," referring to little Johnny Evers of the "Cubs."

"I do, but he's always there," was the mournful reply.

The joke is an old one and told of others. But it's true. Evers, Collins, Wagner, Tinker, a dozen fine short-stops and second basemen are "always there." But even if they were "never there," it isn't one man in a thousand who can "place his hits." Keeler—"Wee Willie"—had the art in such perfection that he could hit to right or left field at will; the incomparable Hal Chase is known as a superb "hit and run" batter, because he can "pull" the ball toward the opening; but the faculty is rare, so rare that it is positive it cannot be developed by practice. It comes naturally or not at all. Therefore, don't bother with it. Hit naturally, hit as nature says you should, and don't bother about "trying to find the holes."

This, of course, doesn't mean you are to place yourself so you always hit fouls or grounders; it does mean that you needn't bother to shift your hands, feet, and bat with every kaleidoscopic change of position by fielders, with the idea that you can "place hit," for generally speaking you can't, and it isn't worth while to spend time trying to do what big League players would give their ears to do, but cannot accomplish.

Learn to hit a long fly; learn to hit a bunt. There is little to be said as to how to learn except what has been stated, "The way to learn to bat is to bat." But knowing how to hit "under the pitch" so as to knock a fly, in distinction to hitting "over the pitch" so as to knock them down on the ground, may be of great value, since a man on third, with less than two out, is a frequent occurrence, and long flies generally are easier to make than are "hits" proper. And the man who cannot bunt when a bunt is the proper thing to play is a handicap to his team. "Laying them down" (a plain, sacrifice bunt) and "poking them out" (a force bunt) are both vital to success in many instances, and he who can "put 'em down the third-base line" or the first-base line, according as there may be a man on first or third, may do more to win than he who can pound out a hit often, and fail when it is most needed.

The real reason why men who hold high batting averages in the minor Leagues fail in major Leagues is not so much the difference in pitching; it is because in minor Leagues a player very often hits for himself, hits the ball he wants to hit. In major Leagues, on the contrary, he has often to hit the ball—or try to—when he is told to hit and not at other times. Consequently, hitting at the ball called for by the manager's signal is vital in practice as well as in games, and you should train yourself to reach for a "wide one" and attempt to knock it down, anyhow, as well as to let such balls go by when it is right to do so. If the catcher "outguesses" you on the "hit and run" signal, and calls for a wide ball, hit it,—hit at it, anyhow,—just to give the runner, who is depending on you, all the aid you can.

Lajoie says, speaking of the "hit and run" play: "Even if I know I am going to miss the ball, I swing hard at it, to cause the catcher to lose a step or a foot or two of ground in making his throw, and in that way help the runner."

Wagner, greatest of batters in the National League, has such control of his bat, such remarkable reach, and such an "eye," that he hits "waste" balls almost as well as fast ones, and no "curves" fool him. They tell a little story of a new pitcher whom a National League team had secured, who had received from some one a little book with notes in it of the kind of balls to pitch to opposing batsmen, according to their habit of batting. The first time he pitched against Pittsburgh, he consulted this book. "Let me see what I must pitch to Wagner," he said, but looked blankly enough at the entry in the little book: "Wagner—give him a base on balls!"

Though you must keep your eye on the pitcher when he pitches, you must learn to look for your signals from the manager or captain, as, even though you may step to the plate with certain instructions, they may be changed after you get there. You must also find time to transmit the signal, if it comes to you, so that the runner will know what you are going to do. For instance, the man ahead of you is on first, and you come to the plate with the orders to hit the third ball, for the "hit and run." But after the second ball is pitched and two balls have been called, your captain has reason to believe the next one will be "wasted," because the other side will *guess* that here is a good chance for you to play the "hit and run." (By "wasting" the ball, the catcher hopes to be able to catch the runner stealing and perhaps help to put you out, too, by having you strike at something from which you can't possibly make a "hit.") So your captain lifts his cap or pats his knee, or whatever the signal may be, and you bang the plate four times with your bat, showing the runner you have been signaled to hit the *fourth* ball pitched.

Signals and signal systems will be taken up in detail later, but get the idea now firmly fixed in your mind that you have other duties at the plate besides merely watching the pitcher and hitting the ball. "Team-work" is all important in batting.

Don't be discouraged if you have a "slump" in your batting record. Larry Lajoie, whose prowess entitles him to consideration when speaking of batting, says a "slump" is all luck. He contends, and with good reason, that if he hits the ball ten days in succession right into various fielders' hands every time, he is a "victim of circumstances." The next ten days he may hit the ball no more and no harder, but they all go just outside some fielder's reach. The first ten days he is reported by the papers as in a "slump"; the next, "batting like a fiend," yet he himself says he has not varied in hitting the ball at any time.

Don't do much "fungo hitting (batting flies with a ball which you toss into the air yourself). It ruins you for batting at fast balls. Note that, in preliminary practice in big Leagues, it is almost invariably a pitcher, who can't hit anyhow, who does the fungo hitting. Why? Because no one else wants to hurt his hitting ability. For the same reason, don't practise batting by hitting at *easy* pitching, merely for the fun of hitting the ball hard. If you learn to hit little easy, soft balls, you train eye and hand for them alone, and when the opposing pitcher is a lad who really can curve them in or send them over fast, you are all at sea.

Old Captain Anson (not old then) when he was at the height of his glory as the greatest batter of his time and the leading light of base-ball, often said that the secret of his ability to lead his League in batting for so many years, was his constant practice day after day, morning after morning, even evening after evening, after the game

He stands with feet wide apart

His "mighty swing"

Hans Wagner

was over, batting, batting, forever batting at the offerings of any one he could get to pitch to him, until the sight of a ball coming towards him to be hit was as familiar as that of the feel of the bat in his hand, and both had become second nature.

Remember, then, the way to learn to bat, flies, bunts, hits, chops, is to bat! Practise, practise, practise. You don't see them, these big Leaguers, but they are at it every day, in the morning, trying to "improve the eye" by practising batting! Practise whenever you can get some one to pitch to you, and strive always to "meet the ball fair," to make a clean hit, rather than to "knock the cover off it," or to "lift it over the fence." Games are won with singles more often than with home runs; the little light man, who seldom hits for extra bases, but who bats to an average .290, is of far more value to his team than the "slugger" who always hits for extra bases when he does hit, but who very seldom makes a hit!

CHAPTER III

Base-Running

Batting, as we have seen, is half the offense in the battle of baseball; base-running is the other half. For no matter how many hits are made, if the runner runs so carelessly that he is put out before he gets home, the hits themselves count for nothing in the final score. And while it is highly important to make hits, it is folly to depend only on hits for the making of runs, and to ignore that part of the art of ball-playing which often turns a few hits into many runs.

But before you can do any base-running, you must get on first base—no matter how. The rules permit a runner making first to overrun the base as far as he will in a straight line and return to it, but do not apply in this way to any other base, which is the reason why sliding is seldom necessary at first and often required at other bases. The slide makes a quick stop possible, and the quick stop is necessary at second and third, but not at first base.

Once started towards first base, and you become a base-runner in the true sense of the word. As soon as you get on first you have several things to do, and all at once.

Not only must you be prepared to advance to second base on the crack of the bat of the man who follows you in the batting order—you must be ready to "steal" second at the first opportunity, to play the "hit and run" on a signal, and at the same time you must watch that you are not "picked off" at first by an alert pitcher, catcher, and first baseman, that you are not the victim of the "hidden-ball" trick, and all the while you must aid the batsman by worrying the pitcher as must as possible, by keeping as long a lead from the base as you can with safety, and drawing as many throws from the pitcher as possible, to tire his arm and distract his attention from the batsman as much as you can.

Only practice will show you how far you can "lead" off first base with the prospects of getting back before the ball gets there when they try to "nip" you. And you can do it much better and farther with some pitchers than with others. Left-handed pitchers are, as a rule, harder to "take a lead from" than right-handers, because they can appear to be going to pitch to the batter when they are actually going to throw to first base, much more easily than can right-handers.

All good pitchers will try to "hold you to the base" by frequent throws to the baseman, which will make you scamper back—perhaps slide back—to the bag. But the instant the ball is returned to the pitcher, you should take your lead again. The more often he has to throw to first, the better for you and the batsman, since every throw distracts his attention from the batter. Moreover, he will have to pitch quickly, and the less time he has to devote to his "motion," the harder it is for him to pitch accurately.

And *watch the ball*! The hidden-ball trick is an example of the importance of watching it. You have a lead from first. The pitcher throws to first, and you make a headlong or feet-first slide for the bag. The first baseman gathers the ball in his mit, and makes a throwing motion with his right hand, but retains the ball in his mit. You on the ground, feel the motion of his arm, or see it, dimly, out of the corner of your eye. You think the ball has been returned to the pitcher and get up and dust yourself off. While doing this, you may step one foot off the bag. "Bang!" and that ball is in you ribs. "Out!" says the umpire—the fans laugh at you, your side scolds you, and the other side chuckles! It is a good plan to stay right where you are, on the bag, until you *see* the ball in the pitcher's hands.

Even old ball-players are fooled with the hidden-ball trick once in a while. Perhaps the most remarkable example of the trick occurred in a game between the "Giants" and "Cubs" in 1910. All base-ball fans know of the "Merkle incident," which will be described at length in a later chapter. For the present, suffice it to say that Merkle, of New York, failed to touch second base in a most important game in 1909, and was called out when Evers, of Chicago, got the ball and claimed a force-out. The decision made the game a tie, and when it was played off, New York lost it, and, by its loss, the pennant. Just a year later in a game with New York, Evers got to first base on a pass, and took his usual dancing lead. The pitcher threw to drive him back to base. Evers slid to the bag, safely enough. Merkle went through the time-worn motion of throwing, holding the ball all the while. Evers got up, shook himself, took his foot from the bag, and—Merkle touched him with the ball, with what satisfaction may be imagined! The umpire saw the play; joy among the fans! It wasn't much of a revenge, from Merkle's standpoint, but the chaffing Evers, the cleverest of players, received for thus being "shown up" must have been balm to Merkle's heart!

The length of your lead from first is governed, too, by the fact of there being a man "on the paths" ahead of you. If there is a man on second while you are on first, the first baseman will play deep or wide—away from his bag. The "play," when it is made, will in all probability be at second or third base. All the defense will try to "get" the leading man, instead of you. Consequently you can play with a much greater lead than when the first baseman is on the bag. But you cannot afford to relax your watchfulness. And here is where the first-base coacher is so handy, for you can watch him and learn where the first baseman is, much more easily than you can watch the baseman.

When you take a lead from second base, the same principles apply. The second baseman and short-stop will neither play close to the bag nor on it, as the first baseman does with only one man "on the paths," and that man on his sack. A pitcher cannot turn completely round and throw to second base to catch a runner off the bag, without giving considerable warning of his intentions. So he won't do it unless you have a big lead. While on first base, you have only the pitcher and catcher to watch—the man with the ball. To see whether or not you are to be "nipped" on second base, you must watch both short-stop and second baseman, pitcher and catcher. You can safely take as long a lead from second base as the nearest player has stepped from it. But just because of your long lead, the pitcher will try to get you by a trick. He will get a signal from somewhere; short-stop or second baseman will run swiftly into the bag; the pitcher will whirl and send the ball almost without looking, and, if you have been "caught napping," you will find the ball waiting for you in the hands of a laughing player whom you thought fifty feet away! So watch the baseman, the short-stop, the third-base coacher, and the pitcher, when you take a long lead for third.

And don't forget that little, seldom-needed, but vital rule of base-ball, "A base-runner struck with a batted ball is out." Watch the ball when it is hit. If it's a grounder crossing your path, see that it doesn't hit your legs. Jump over it, wait for it to go by, do anything, but don't let it touch you. But once the ball is by you—forget it. Put your head down and *run*! Don't try to see where the ball has gone, unless it is a fly. Depend on the coachers. They are there for that purpose. The fraction of a second it takes you to look over your

Successful steal home

shoulder for the ball may mean the difference between "safe" and out. And don't run on high flies more than half-way—be *sure* the fly isn't going to be caught before you tear round the bases, unless, of course, there are two out, when it makes no difference, since, if the ball is caught, the side is out, and if it isn't caught, you may score if you can beat the ball. Hence, with two out, *run*, whether the ball is a fly or a grounder.

When you run more than one base at a time, you must remember that the fraction of a second which you may lose or gain, *en route*, by any calculation, speed, skill, or the lack of them, means the difference between good and "bone-head" base-running. The mere matter of turning the bag, that is, rounding the corner, may have a vital importance.

Johnson has just released a curve

Johnson has just finished pitching

Walter Johnson of Washington (American League), the beloved "Idaho Wonder," whose speed is said to be greater than that of Amos Rusie

Stretching a one-base hit into a two-bagger, or a two-bagger into three, running wild on the bases, in other words, is spectacular, and frequently good base-ball. In this game, as in every other athletic game, daring, courage, and nerve often succeed. The very unexpectedness of the attempt to get an extra base, even where it looks foolhardy, will often insure success. But there are times when spectacular base-ball, even if successful, is foolish. For instance, what good is it to make second base, by a hair, on a *single*, when there are two out, in the ninth inning, and a big score against you? In such circumstances, the *only* thing which can help is a batting rally, and if the next man "at bat" is going to start the rally, you are just as well off on first as on second. And, by stretching your single into a double, you run a great risk of being, yourself, the third "out," and thus nipping all chances for a rally!

But, if the score were tied, or you were only one or two runs behind, that is a time to play the spectacular game—to run the extra base—to take instant advantage of every careless move. "Ty" Cobb, the famous Detroit outfielder, the most spectacular base-runner in either League, frequently gets put out, taking chances. But, much more frequently, he "makes good" with his long chances, and turns scratches into singles, singles into doubles, and doubles into triples and home runs by his bold playing.

An instance when daring base-running succeeded by its unexpectedness was presented in the second game of the World's Series of 1910 between the Champion Chicago "Cubs" and the Champion Philadelphia Athletics. The "Cubs" had scored and were ahead up to the third inning—strange to say, the Athletics were encouraged by being scored upon, since they had well noted throughout the year that whenever Coombs, who was pitching that day, was scored upon early in the contest, he invariably won. In the third inning, the Athletics had Thomas on third, Lord on first, and two out. Collins, the whirlwind second baseman of the Athletics, was at bat. He sent a sharp line-drive just inside third base, and reached second base. Thomas, of course, scored. Every one expected Lord, who had come from first base, to stop on third, as the ball was already on its way to Steinfeldt, Chicago's third baseman, from the outfield. But Lord kept right on, full-tilt, for the plate. "Steiny," taken by surprise, made a desperate effort to touch Lord, and—dropped the ball! Lord scored, and the Athletics were not headed thereafter in that game!

The question of stealing bases—which is the best part of the art of base-running, and the most spectacular feature of the game—is one to be considered from more than one point of view. The average young ball-player, if you ask him when he should steal a base, will probably answer, "Any time you get a chance!" But unless he qualified the "any" time with the words "good chance," he would be wrong. "Inside ball" teaches players that base-stealing must be considered with reference to the score, to the number of innings yet to be played, the number of men out at the time, and the batting order. For instance, with a man on first and third, the temptation for the man on first to steal second is very strong. He knows he can take a big lead, because the first baseman will be playing for the batter, and not for him. He knows that if he can draw a throw from the catcher to second base at a time when the man on third has a good lead toward home, and make the bag, the man on third will probably be successful in stealing home, making the play a double steal. But suppose two men are out? Then if the stealer from first base is caught, the side is out, and the run does not count. If it is the eighth or ninth inning, and a run is needed to tie the score or win the game, and the batter is weak, then the attempt to steal second with two out, and a man on third, may be justifiable, since the situation is acute. But if the batter is strong, then it may be unwise to risk the steal, because you know all the attention will be directed to getting *you*, coming in to second, and it is at least possible that the man at bat will make a hit, scoring the man on third.

With less than two out, the man on first should always try to steal with a man on third, for then the attention of the defense will be largely directed to the man on third base, and your chances of getting second base are good. If they try to put *you* out at second, the man on third is almost sure to score; if they hold *him* to *his* bag, *you* are almost certain to be safe at second! The defense to this play will be taken up later, but, in considering it now as an offensive play and part of good base-running, always remember to think of the number of men who are out, the probabilities of the man at the bat making a hit—which includes his previous performance against the opposing pitcher—the score, and whether the situation is normal, desperate, or just balanced between, and govern your actions accordingly.

The base-runner who gets on first and just waits to be "batted round" the circuit is playing very safe, but very poor base-ball. The standard play, with no score, and a man on first, is a sacrifice hit—if you can steal second, the sacrifice will put you on third instead, with but one man out! And if one man is out, and you are on first, and no one else is "on," how important to steal second, so that your side's situation is no worse than if you had been sacrificed to second! If two are out, you simply *must* steal second, unless heavy hitters follow you, whose prospects are good for a hit, otherwise it is almost certain the side will be retired without a score. If the score is heavily against you near the end of the game, a stolen base or so is of little value; it takes heavy hitting and lots of it to make up that lead you are struggling against. If the lead is but one or two runs, however, then your case is desperate but full of hope, and a certain recklessness and chance-taking is indicated on the paths.

How important a steal of second may be is shown by the record of the fourth game in the World's Series for 1910. Sheckard, the hard-hitting, fast-running left-fielder of the Chicago "Cubs," drew a base on balls, and while Schulte, of Chicago, was busily engaged in striking out, Sheckard stole second base cleanly. Of course the crowd went crazy. But they had something better to get crazy about the next minute, for Sheckard scored on Hofman's single. In other words, a score resulted from a pass and a lone hit, *because* Sheckard stole second! The next two men were out in short order. Had Sheckard not stolen that base, but waited for Hofman's single to advance him to second, he would have died there, and the inning been without a score. As the final score was four to three, in favor of Chicago, on that one stolen base the winning of the game depended. Had that run not been made, the contest might have had to go many extra innings, instead of the one extra it did go, and while the result might have been the same—it might have been different! In which case the humiliation for Chicago of the Athletics' winning four straight games in a World's Championship would have happened!

Do you imagine the Chicago fans approved of Sheckard? Well, rather.

Stealing third is less often accomplished than stealing second, for several reasons—the shorter distance from catcher to third base compared with the distance from catcher to second base being one, and the fact that this act of piracy usually succeeds only through sheer audacity, being another. To offset this is the larger lead you can take from second base. It will largely depend on where the third baseman is playing, whether or not you can try to steal third. If he is playing in for a bunt, you have a better chance than if he is playing deep, since, if playing in, he cannot as well see you coming nor get back to the bag to take the throw from the catcher as quickly as he can see and run in when playing deep. On the other hand, the score and the innings and the number of men out must be considered in steal-

Caught off second base

"Out, on first!" A close decision

ing third, just as in stealing second, only if two are out, it makes less difference whether you steal third or not than it would if you were on first and wanted second. You can probably score from second, if you are fast, on any real hit—and you cannot score from third on a "third out" anyhow.

Stealing home is a fascinating play. It has two variations—one the "squeeze" play, which will be taken up later, and the other, the straight steal of home. It may be accomplished at times when a pitcher takes a long "wind-up"—it may be when a passed ball or a wild pitch allows you to gain the plate (although under such circumstances, of course, you do not get credit for a "steal"), or it may be by sheer speed and nerve, surprising the catcher so that you slide right into his feet even while he has the ball, before he thinks to touch you. But it is a risky play, and is for either a very desperate situation indeed, as when two are out, and it is almost certain the batter will strike out, or when you are so far in the lead you can afford to take chances.

Stealing any base is often done on slow catchers by watching them and seeing when they throw back the ball to the pitcher slowly or carelessly. The steal then becomes a "delayed steal"—you have delayed it until the catcher is off his guard. Another form of "delayed steal" which not infrequently succeeds, is that accomplished by taking a big lead from first, on a run, stopping short just for an instant, drawing the throw from the catcher to first, and then diving for second! It is then a race between you and the second baseman or shortstop—the first baseman cannot throw the ball until some one is on the second bag to take the throw, and unless both first baseman and man covering the second bag work like clockwork, the chances are you can slide into second safely.

Double steals are what their name implies—a stealing of two bases at once. Of course, when the man ahead of you steals, it is folly for you not to do so also, since they cannot put you both out at once, unless by the finest kind of a double play. This applies to the double steal of a second and third, and not second and home, since, as previously described, the stealing of second with third occupied may be permitted by the defense rather than risking the man on third making a score with the double steal.

Triple steals are so rare in major League base-ball that less than half a dozen have ever been made! The Philadelphia Nationals made one in 1910 against Cincinnati, and players talk of it yet. It was in the first inning. Grant was on third, Magee on second, and "Kitty" Bransfield on first. Fromme was pitching for Cincinnati, and he had an unusually long wind-up. Grant had hesitated for an instant, on his running lead for home, two or three times, and had scuttled back to third when Fromme looked at him, ball under his chin. But the instant Fromme started the long wind-up, Grant ducked his head and ran, Magee started for third, and Bransfield for second. Fromme let the ball go, and McLean made a clean catch, but Grant slid right under the throw, scoring, and by the time McLean straightened up it was too late to catch either of the other runners. Other triple steals have been made by St. Louis against the Athletics in 1905, by the Athletics against Washington in 1908, and by Boston against the Athletics in 1909.

Triple steals are so rare for many reasons, one being their difficulty, another the fact that they are not tried with two men out; three men "on," and only one or none out, is not a common situation! A third reason is that the chance of making a two- or three-run inning of it, if a hit results, is always a hope when the bases are full, whereas a triple steal, if it fails, may mean the retiring of the side.

One of the most vital things to learn in the art of base-running is sliding—how to slide and when to slide. There are numerous slides: the feet-first slide, the head-first slide, the wide slide, the "hook" slide, the "fall away" slide, et cetera.

The wide slide is usually taken head first. You slide wide of second, and half-way past it, and reach out and grab the bag with your left hand. It is useful in this way: it makes it very hard for the baseman to find any portion of you to touch with the ball! The "hook" slide is similar in intent, but in it you come in feet first, and either sitting or lying down. The bag is caught with one outstretched foot instead of the hand.

Note well that you had best slide to the *right* and *outside* of the base when the ball comes from *within* the diamond, and to the *left* and *inside* the base when the ball comes from the *outfield*. In this way you come into the bag *behind* the man on the bag, and require him to turn around to touch you. It is just such little points that mean the tiny fraction of a second which spells the difference between safety and a walk to the bench.

As an indication of how hard it is to steal a base against a good team, and how much, therefore, in practice and patience in all departments, particularly in stealing, the art calls for, consider the records for 1910. In the National League, Bescher, of Cincinnati, led all the players with 70 stolen bases for the year. These he pilfered in 150 games, less than "half a base" per game. In the American League, Collins, of Philadelphia, purloined 81 bases in 153 games, a little more than "half a base" per game.

The Cincinnati "Reds," in the National League, as a team, had the greatest number of stolen bases to their credit for the year, 310 secured in 156 games, a fraction less than two bases per game. The New York "Highlanders" led in the American League with 284 stolen bases in 156 games. And because the chances of the expert stealer are so evenly balanced against the expert of defense, the stolen base is, and always will be, one of the charms of base-ball, always recognized as a great feat by the crowds, and appreciated by players as something hard to do.

One more point, and we are through with the elementary survey of the art of base-running—when caught between bases, stay alive as long as you can, particularly when you are not alone "on the paths." Then, if there is a runner ahead of you, strive to draw the throws from the two men running you down, by dodging back and forth, in the hope that in the confusion he may score or at least advance a base. If he is behind you, strive to be caught, if caught you must be, at the farthest base you can, so that there is the less chance to make a double play on the other man, and so that he, too, may steal a base. And if there is no one on the paths, and you are caught, don't give up easily. Dodge. Duck. Turn. Twist. *Fight* for your base—for the same reason you "run everything out."

CHAPTER IV

Generalship of Offense

Let it be understood at the start that there can be nothing "cut and dried" about base-ball. You cannot write a formula for generalship. Circumstances alter cases. What is right in one situation may be wrong in another, even though both situations appear the same. If base-ball could be reduced to a mathematical problem, if it could always be worked out to such a certainty that, given X pitching a fast ball, waist-high, Y batting, and Z on second, a run would always result, the game would have little interest. It is the unexpectedness of the contest, the fact that "the game isn't over until the last man's out," that makes it so fine a sport.

So any account of generalship, designed to be instructive, must be considered as suggestive only, and certainly not to be regarded as were the laws of the Medes and the Persians.

There is the "hit-and-run" play, for instance. When shall a manager order it tried? When can it be expected to aid, when hinder, the chances of a run? The decision rests with the general directing the game, yet not infrequently, no matter what he decides, the game confutes him. But it is undeniable that bad generalship loses almost as many games as bad playing.

Earl Wagner, one-time President of the Washington Base-ball

The "Hit-and-Run"
But they don't always hit it!

Club in the old National League days, used to say, "Mechanical errors by players are mere incidents of the game—tactical errors are its features and by them games are won and lost."

As all base-ball fans know, the hit-and-run play is tried with a man on first base and usually with less than two out—it may be one or none out. When the hit-and-run play is signaled, the runner starts for second base the instant the pitcher draws his arm back for the pitch. The batter strives to hit that pitched ball, whether it be good or bad, high or low. The play has several angles and possibilities. If the batter hits the ball so that it goes straight into some infielder's

"Blocked Off!"
(Note the runner's cap in the air)

hands, he is out, and the runner is also out, barring an error, since the ball can be thrown to first base long before the runner can turn and get back. If the batter knocks a high fly, the base-runner must pull up and watch to see if it is caught—if it is, the batter is out and the runner must hurry back to first base. But if the batter hits a grounder, the chances are good that both he and the runner will be safe, the batter on first, the runner on second, or *third*, which possibility is the object of the play. And if the batter misses the ball entirely, the runner has an excellent chance of making a straight steal. The whole effort of the latter should be to hit the ball to right field and on the ground, or low—hence a good base-ball general will not order the hit-and-run with a man at bat who generally hits to left field or straight over second base.

The batter wants to knock the ball to right field for two reasons. The first is that the second baseman, seeing the runner start to steal second, will be in duty bound to cover the second bag. The gap thus left between the second and first baseman is wide, and a grounder which would ordinarily be "gobbled up" by the second baseman rolls safe. The second reason is that if the batted ball is fast and low, the man running to second may easily make third base, also, whereas if the ball went through short-stop, the runner could not get to third before the leftfielder could get it and return it to third base. The whole function of the play hinges on these things, and the possibility of putting a man on third base, from first, on a "single."

The good field general ordinarily will not order the hit-and-run with a slow runner on first, when the pitcher "holds" the runner well to first base; with a poor batter "up"; with a batter up who hits to left field; with two out; or when he is being "outguessed" by the defense. For instance, with two balls and no strikes, a man on first and none out, the hit-and-run is often played, since it is probable the pitcher will try to "cut the plate" on his third pitch. The defense knows this. But in this situation, just because it is unexpected, a "pitch out" is often ordered by the catcher—that is, the pitcher is to deliver the ball "wide" of the plate, so that the catcher can make a perfect catch and throw to second, to catch the runner, preventing the batter from hitting the ball at all. So the good general will attempt to catch the "pitch out" signal, and flash *his* countermand of the hit-and-run order, thus making the pitcher "waste" a ball, and keeping the runner "tied" to his base, preventing his being put out. The beauty of base-ball generalship is seen right here in the outguessing of the opposing general and compelling the pitcher to "get in a hole," i.e., pitch several "balls" instead of "strikes," so that, to avoid passing the batter to first, he is *compelled* to "put one over" the plate, thus giving the batter an excellent chance to make a hit. The hit-and-run play is thus often signaled without being actually played—an obvious signal to play the hit-and-run, secretly countermanded, to get the pitcher to waste balls, being a very effective play and in the end often producing a safe hit or an advance of runners as well as if the play itself were successfully tried.

The "squeeze play" is on the same plan as the hit-and-run, but played with a runner on third base instead of first. It is never played with two out, unless the side playing it is so far in the lead that any sort of a chance may be taken for the fun of it. The runner on third takes as big a lead as he dares, and sprints for the plate with the pitcher's motion. The batter tries only to "meet" the ball—he doesn't want to take chances hitting it, or try to drive it anywhere—he wants simply to touch it and prevent the catcher from getting it. For the runner is coming in to the plate so fast that if the ball rolls ten feet from the bat, the chances of his getting across the "rubber" before the ball can be fielded by either catcher or pitcher are excellent.

But if the batter fails to hit the ball, the runner is made to look very foolish indeed, since he comes up the plate to find the waiting catcher, with the ball in his hands, ready to "put it on him." In the hit-and-run, if the batter fails to hit, the runner may well make a straight steal of second, for the catcher must throw one hundred and twenty feet, the baseman must catch the ball and tag the runner, before he is out. In the "squeeze," the catcher doesn't have to throw the ball at all, he has it ready and waiting. But in the hit-and-run, a batter who *bunts* makes of his play but an ordinary sacrifice play—he is probably put out at first easily, and the runner has little chance of making third base. Whereas the *bunter* in the *squeeze* may easily be safe, since the fielded ball may be thrown to the plate in an attempt to put out the runner, and, even if the batter is put out at first, a run has scored, and he is happy.

The good general will not ordinarily order a squeeze with a good *hitter* up, preferring the chance of his making a "hit," or with a slow runner on third, when his side is ahead of the game, unless he is so far ahead he is willing to take chances, or perhaps with the bases filled, the one time in a thousand when it is wise to try a triple steal. But with a good *bunter* up, two or three balls on the pitcher, a fast man on third, and a run badly needed, it may be a first-class play to try. It is also indicated when the pitcher is easily "rattled," for, seeing the man tearing in from third, he may throw wild to the catcher.

The "sacrifice advance," more often called the sacrifice bunt, is the usual, average, general play with a man on first and none out. The offense figures they can afford to lose a man "out" at first to advance the man on first base to second base, particularly with the batting order "right"—that is, with the fast man on first, the good bunter or sacrifice hitter at bat, and the "clean up" man, noted for long drives and a good batting average, "on deck," that is, next "at bat." For with a man on second, one out, and two hitters coming (the result of the sacrifice advance), the chances of a score are good.

Yet the wise general, knowing the defense *expects* the ordinary, average play, will often order a hit-and-run, or a straight steal. For if he can have a man on second and *none* out, there is no limit to the things he may do—his chances of scoring are so much greater with only two bases to run and three batters coming, that he may depend entirely from there on, on sacrifice hitting, or he may get a man on first while the man on second is held to his bag and try a double steal, or a double delayed steal—so that here, as elsewhere, the sacrifice advance, though common, usual, and successful many times, may be—should be—varied occasionally by a keen general, to the confusion of the defense.

Stealing second or third—double steals, delayed steals, triple steals, already spoken of in the paper on base-running—may be opportunities taken by players, or ordered from the bench. The good general will not order a steal of second with none out and a slow runner "on," if a fine batter is "up," but he will order it with one or two out, if the conditions of batting order, the kind of pitcher, and the state of the game warrant it. Left-handed pitchers, who usually hold players well to their bases, may be subjects for the *delayed* steal, in which the man on first takes a dancing lead, while the catcher has the ball, and who, poising for a sprint and slide back to first, makes it hard for the catcher to decide whether to throw to first base or return the ball to the pitcher. If he does the latter, the runner, "pulling off" the delayed steal, will start for second base as hard as he can go the instant the catcher tosses the ball to the pitcher. The pitcher, surprised, and not in position to whirl and make the throw to second in the minimum of time—caught "flat-footed" as ball-players say—will often get the ball to second base too late to catch the runner. Not infrequently he has to "hold his throw," waiting for the equally surprised second baseman or short-stop to get to the base in time to catch the ball. The "delayed steal" is thus a strategic move involving surprise of the enemy as its most salient feature, and the good base-ball general will take into consideration the wariness of his opponents and the character of the men on the paths and infield, before ordering it. He will also try to know what kind of a ball is to be pitched, and what the defense is going to do. It is largely a guessing-match, and yet it is guessing, and guessing right, which wins games.

This "guessing-match" is often intricate and involved. There is an instance often reported by admirers of the Chicago "Cubs" in

One Tenth of a Second Counts
And the runner is out!

which Frank Chance, the captain, repeatedly outguessed the "Reds" (Cincinnati), with which team they were playing a hard game. Chance had the "acute situation" to deal with, a man on first and another on third. Roth, catching for Cincinnati, signaled his pitcher for a curve ball. Chance guessed that a curve was coming and ordered a delayed double steal, figuring that the batter would miss the curve and that the Cincinnati catcher, elated at a "strike," would be less watchful in returning the ball and the pitcher less keenly on the look-out for a steal in getting ready for his next pitch. But some one of the "Reds" saw the signal, the team shifted its position, and got up on tiptoe.

One Tenth of a Second Counts
And, this time, the runner is safe!

Their signal was changed and a "pitch out" called for. Kane, coaching for Chicago, noted as a "signal reader," saw the "pitch out" signal and Chance changed *his* orders. His runners held their bases, and a ball was "wasted." On the next ball, Chance again ordered the delayed double steal. Roth guessed it, and ordered another "pitch out." Chance saw this, and ordered a wait. Roth saw the change and ordered a fast, high ball. Chance, guessing he would do so, suddenly ordered a hit-and-run, a daring thing to do, a base hit was made, two runs scored, and the game was over!

Beware the hit-and-run with first and second occupied—the grave danger of the play is a line ball to the infield resulting in a triple play, thus: the line ball, caught, puts the batter out; the first baseman, who makes the catch, steps to the initial bag, putting the first base occupant out (he having run for second); the first baseman throws to second base, in ample time to get the runner from that station who has run for third and hasn't had time to get back. In the same way, a ground ball, which has to be fielded to first base to get the runner, may be sent to second base to catch the man coming in, or to third to catch the man coming from second. In other words, the hit-and-run, with two men on, not only increases the chance of a score, but of retiring the side. Therefore, consider, before ordering it. Moreover, the "gap" between first and second basemen is not so wide when the hit-and-run is tried with two bases occupied, for all the attention of the defense will be devoted to getting the leading runner.

Generally speaking, the squeeze is not tried with the bases full, and the simple, unassisted triple steal is markedly rare. It requires complete coöperation between all three runners, and a fast man on third trying to get home.

But the vital situation, that productive of the most interest in a ball game, is when first and third are occupied. The plays were discussed in the last paper—but what to do as captain, general, manager, when to order the single steal of second, in the hope of getting the man on third a chance to come home, when to order the double steal straight or delayed, both starting at once—those are hard questions. But, if this problem is hard for the general of the offense, it is ten times as hard for the general of the defense, and so the offensive general may well wait on his decision and see what happens. It is generally conceded that desperate situations require desperate remedies—if the game is far gone and you are far behind, it is foolish to try to have the man on first steal second—the defense will play for him, and let the run score, since it can't hurt them, but a long-continued game can. On the other hand, if you are but a run or so behind, the situation may well be so acute that the defense will not play for the runner on first at all, but will devote their attention to the man on third—hence it is wise to order the steal of second. There is always the chance that they *will* play for this runner, letting the run score, and if they don't, why, you are a base ahead and the succeeding batsman has a chance of two runs in a hit from his bat, instead of one!

The good base-ball general will never hesitate to change the men on his team when the necessities arise. If a pitcher is to be taken out of the game and another substituted, a "pinch hitter" is frequently sent into the game between the two. Thus, A is pitching, but is to retire in favor of B. C, a pinch-hitter, gets in the game first, takes A's place, and hits for him, and then B takes C's place and pitches for him. It is a rule of the game that a man taken out cannot play again in that game, consequently, one man is never substituted for another who is not definitely through for that day.

A few well-understood signals must be learned thoroughly, in the offense as well as the defense. You may arrange that these signals be given verbally or by motions, but they must be clear and well understood. The base-ball general must have a signal, with his batters and runners, for the hit-and-run, which will also serve for the squeeze; for stealing a base, which will serve for the double and triple steals, also, since, of course, if a steal is ordered, all the men "on" will steal; for the delayed steal; for a sacrifice play, and for a bunt.

Your signals may be words or deeds. You may scratch your nose for a single steal, or take off your cap for a hit-and-run. Or you may work into your coacher's talk a quiet, "Not yet; not yet, *George*," and your runner will know that the use of his name means a steal. Your batter may be instructed to try the hit-and-run by being audibly commanded to do something else, as "Hit 'er out" for a try on the *third* ball, "Hit her" for a try on the *second* ball, "Hit—you, Jack" for the play on the *first* ball, and so forth. Or you may instruct him simply to try the hit-and-run, and use his judgment as to the ball on which he will play it, whereupon he must signal the runner what ball he will try to hit, which he may do by hitting the plate, once, twice, thrice or four times with his bat, or rubbing his right hand on his trousers, the number of fingers exposed showing the runner the number of the ball he will have to run on.

But beware the signal which is too easy to give, and which may, in a moment of forgetfulness, be given without intending it as a signal at all. In a game between Rochester and Buffalo, such a mix up once occurred, at the cost of the game. The Rochester manager used a set of signals which were all "natural" movements—that is, they consisted of putting the hand on the hip, lifting the cap, crossing the feet, etc., etc., instead of verbal calls with concealed meanings. These signals were often given by some one designated player on the bench, the better to avoid their being detected, for, of course, it soon becomes apparent that a team is using a set of silent signals and the managers and coaches are closely watched by the opposition to see if these signals can be detected.

In this particular game, Dan Coogan, Rochester catcher, was the signal man. The score was a tie, and excitement was intense. Smith, of Rochester, got to first base on a hit. He glanced at Coogan, sitting on the bench, observed his feet crossed, which was the signal that day for a steal, and promptly dashed for second base, reaching that station safely and in a cloud of dust.

A base hit now would win the game. But to the horror of the spectators and the indignation of the manager, Smith dashed for third on the first ball pitched, and was neatly retired there, catcher to third baseman.

"Who told you to steal?" vociferated the indignant manager!

"Who told you to steal second and why did you try to steal third? I pay you to obey orders, not throw away ball games—etc., etc., etc."

Smith was equally indignant. "I stole because I was ordered!" he shouted. "I'm not running this ball game. Look—there's Coogan, and his feet are crossed yet"; and off he stalked in high dudgeon, and the manager turned his attention to the innocent Coogan, who, quite forgetting the importance of the signal, his work not usually being that of signal giver, had been sitting with his feet, one on top of the other, wondering what in the world had thrown his usually level-headed captain off his balance!

Perhaps the utmost perfection in signaling, both in offense and defense, was reached when the Chicago "Cubs," the great base-ball machine built up and perfected by Frank Chance, the "Peerless Leader," were the World's Champions. Manager Chance, of course, changed signals frequently. One of his signals for a steal was given by changing positions with some one on the bench. When he got up and looked over the bats on the ground, his runners and batsmen knew a hit-and-run was ordered. Sometimes he ordered double steals by lifting his cap; again, his signals would be calls to his players, in which "Hofman" might mean "steal on the first ball"; "Steiny" (short for Steinfeldt), "hit-and-run"; "Sheckard," "bunt toward third," etc.

Planning signals is easy—practising them and learning them not hard, but both are vital to the offense, as well as the defense, although defensive signals are greater in number than the offensive signals. In other words, to hit, to run, to score, is all the offense can do. But the defense, to put men out at any of three bases and home, can have any one of a hundred combinations at work to trap a runner, and needs many more signals to instruct nine men what to do than does the offense, which has never more than four men in the game at once.

The opposing team will try to steal your signals—will, by watching everything you do and say and the immediately following play, try to frustrate your offense. It is part of the game. And just for that reason, you should have several sets of signals, for offense, which you can use without confusion. Thus, you should have an audible set, a visual set, a coacher's set, perhaps two of each. They need not be complicated or hard to learn. If there are too many signals to learn, players may get the several sets confused, and confusion in signals means getting beaten! Hence, have your signals as few as possible and as simple as possible, but have several sets so you can change if you find the other general has read your signals and is anticipating what you are going to do. And do you, in your turn, watch your opponent, in *his* offense, and see if *you* can detect any connection between his acts, his speech, and the things his runners do. Watch his defensive signals, too, for if you can learn what the pitch is to be, and tell, by the shifting of the infield and the outfield, what they expect you to do, you can perhaps do something else. Be particular to try to get the catcher's signals, and to learn what the pitcher is going to do by watching him—with a man on base, to know when a waste ball is coming is invaluable since the more balls you can make a pitcher "waste" in the endeavor to catch a man stealing who *won't* steal, the more likely you are to make him put the ball over the plate in the end.

But the highest part of generalship is in the planning of the game—the campaign itself. A manager who can do this well wins many games before they are played. Briefly, such a planning beforehand means discovering an opponent's weakness, and playing to it. Thus, in 1909, the general plan of the Boston American League team was to run—run when they should and when they shouldn't—run whether they got put out or not—run, run, run. Their whole idea was that speed won ball games. Their nickname was the Boston "Speed

The Catcher Giving His Signals

"Sliding In" under the Catcher

Boys." They ran wildly, foolishly, wisely, speedily—but they always ran. The result was they threatened to win a pennant by running! But other managers finally decided to let them run! And consistent "pitching out" and good throwing by catchers finally stopped them.

Now if you have a team to play which has a weak-throwing catcher, plan your games on the idea of stealing second base every time you can, then third base, a little more cautiously; try to make as many scores on as few hits as you can—run, as the Boston Speed Boys did, and see if the weak-throwing catcher can stop you. If, on the contrary, the catcher is strong, but the pitcher weak, plan your game on bunts and hits—don't try to steal, play "straight base-ball," and let the batter bat the runner 'round. If the pitcher is weak on fielding, bunt and run, bunt and run, bunt and run, and while sometimes he will get you, at other times you will beat the ball, and few things demoralize a pitcher more than trying to do swift fielding which doesn't succeed or goes utterly "wild."

McCloskey, when managing the St. Louis Cardinals, restrained his team from hitting the ball in a game with Chicago, when Reulbach was pitching, making his men bunt, bunt, bunt. They didn't want to bunt—they wanted to hit. And they bunted themselves out of the game for six innings, the infield making those bunts count for "outs" in rapid succession. But in the seventh, two bunts went safe, a sacrifice bunt advanced them, a bunt to first base was thrown wild to the plate, two runs scored, the Chicago players were in a rout, and before the ninth inning was over, McCloskey's players had "bunted out" five runs!

If the pitcher is very strong, and you have the nerve, do as Chance did when the "Cubs" played Detroit for the Championship of the World and beat them, and make your whole team "wait out" a pitcher. It was the second game of the last series between these two teams, played before a huge crowd. When Chicago learned that "Wild

Bill" Donovan was to pitch for Detroit, Chance issued his single order "wait."

The team waited. Inning after inning passed—no score. The crowd yelled, shrieked, groaned for a hit—but the team waited. Man after man went to the plate and waited—took as many balls as he could get, made as many fouls as he could, got his two strikes—often his three strikes—and gave place to the next man. When a man did get on first base he did his best to draw throws from Donovan, anything to get him to throw and tire him out. "Wait," said Chance when his men begged to be allowed to hit. "Wait. The time hasn't come yet; wait!" And they waited, those "Cubs," like hounds held in leash, impatient to be off, crazy to drive one of those teasing curves, those cannon-ball fast ones, out of the lot.

They waited until the eighth inning. Hofman led off. He led off with a vengeance and a safe hit. Chance knew the time had come. "Hit it, Tinker," he said, and Tinker, smiling and drawing a deep breath, stepped to the plate. He was free. He could hit any ball he pleased! And the first one pleased him mightily, and he smote it to the far outfield until it hit the fence. And others followed him, and they were also free, and they also picked out the balls that "Wild Bill" sent toward them, and smote each man the kind he liked the best, and when the smoke of battle cleared away, the "Cubs," well fed with runs, totaled six for their score, and the game was won.

It was won by Chance, who figured that Donovan, unhittable when "right," would "pitch his arm off" if made to pitch enough, and that then, before Jennings, manager for Detroit, could switch pitchers, a few hits in succession would win the game. It won it.

Never confuse signaling with generalship. Never use a signal when plain instructions will do. If you want to play the hit-and-run, tell the batter so before he goes to the plate, and let him signal the runner—don't wait until he is at the plate, and signal the runner, and have him signal the batter. The simplest way is the best. Chance *told*, not signaled, his men to "wait." And just because the captain or manager can talk to his players on the offense, except when he himself is "on the paths," he needs much fewer signals for offensive work than for defensive work.

And don't try to do it all from the bench. It isn't always possible to exercise generalship—sometimes the best planning is found in letting the man at bat and on the base do what seems to him best. Sometimes an opportunity to steal will occur which no manager could foresee, or order—the "signal-ridden" player, who looks to his manager for everything, would never take the opportunity—a man like Cobb, alert to every opportunity, will take the chance and make his steal, and then look to see what his general wants him to do next!

A delayed-double-steal bit of generalship was described in the first chapter. Another instance, this time a single delayed steal, almost as spectacular, although less depended on it, occurred in a game between the Pittsburgh "Pirates" and the Philadelphia "Phillies" last year. Wagner was on second base, one out. He got the signal for a delayed steal and danced away from second so far that it looked as if he must be caught. But "Red" Dooin, the captain and great catcher of the "Phillies," knows what a base-runner Wagner is, and he wasn't to be tricked. He drew back his arm to throw, and paused. Wagner danced back toward second base. Dooin made as if to throw to the pitcher. Wagner danced off second again. Again Dooin's arm poised for the throw, and again Wagner waited. Four times did Dooin "bluff" the throw to second base, and four times Wagner took chances—but could not draw the throw. Then, apparently giving it up, he took a short lead only. But those who were near him tell of seeing his great muscles set, and when Dooin, deceived at last, carelessly tossed the ball back to his pitcher, Wagner was off like a flash, slid in under the third baseman, and although the pitcher was quick, the third

Caught Between Third Base and Home

baseman couldn't *quite* get the ball at the right time—and Wagner was "safe." No manager could order all that. It requires some brains in the "how" of obedience, as well as a training to obey absolutely, in base-ball as in warfare.

McGraw, now manager of the New York "Giants," and "Wee Willie" Keeler, perhaps the most artistic batsman who ever played the game, would never have established their freak record of two runs on a base on balls and a short single, if they had waited for orders

The Fallaway Slide

from the bench. Both were with Baltimore, in the Old National League, playing the "Senators," as the National League Washington team was called, in the capital city. McGraw drew a base on balls. Keeler came to bat, flashed the hit-and-run signal to him, hoping, by hitting to right field, to let McGraw get to third base. But Keeler made a mistake, or the pitch took an odd curve, or something went wrong, for he hit to *left* field. McGraw, of course, had started for second as the ball was pitched. Abbey, in left field for the "Senators" (Washington), naturally thought McGraw would stop at second, never dreaming he would try for third when the ball was already in his (Abbey's) hands. McGraw figured on this, and did try for third.

Abbey threw lazily enough to third base, McGraw twisted away in his slide, and was "safe." Meanwhile, of course, Keeler had kept on to second, seeing the ball and McGraw racing each other to third.

McGraw, guessing that Joyce, the third baseman, was *sure* he, McGraw, was through, got up and sprinted for home as Joyce turned to pick up the ball from the ground. Joyce, rattled, threw wild to the catcher, and McGraw scored. And as he picked himself out of the dust he was all but knocked down by little "Wee Willie" Keeler shooting in through the dirt and over the plate, behind him. It was daring, crazily daring, base-running, but it won a game by two runs on a base on balls and a short single—something for which there is no parallel in major League base-ball history.

It was a play, or series of plays, impossible to order from the bench, yet it showed generalship of the highest class. And it is that generalship on the part of McGraw which makes the "Giants" so hard to beat to-day, and which keeps them always dangerous, even to the last moment, in any game they play.

Chapter V

Defense—Pitcher and Catcher

Defensive "inside ball" begins with the pitcher and the catcher. Detailed descriptions of the various "deliveries" which generations of pitchers have developed, and instructions by which boys can imitate them, can be found in most base-ball manuals, but it can be said here that while a repertoire of curves, fast balls, "spit balls," slow ones," a "fade-away," a "drop," a "jump," and a "wide curve" ball, is a very useful thing for a pitcher to possess, the vast majority of major League pitchers do not try to master all known kinds of delivery, but stick to a few and learn them thoroughly. Different men have different ways of pitching a ball naturally, and a pitcher's development is usually best made along easy, natural lines, even though base-ball history is full of men like "Big Six" Mathewson, of the New York "Giants," who, late in his pitching career, patiently and slowly developed a new delivery which he could throw only after hours of hard practice. This is the famous "fade-away," the terror and despair of most batters who have to face it.

The acquired curves—those which do not come naturally—may well be let alone by boys, for this reason: a boy's arm is a growing arm.

Both bones and muscles are not what they will be in manhood. Pitching a ball which strains the arm when it is young and growing, may fatally injure it for fine pitching when it has its growth. While not one lad in a hundred who reads this expects to be a professional base-ball player, there may be also not one in a hundred who does not expect to play base-ball at intervals for some time to come. Moreover, straining an arm may keep you from pitching *now* as well as later; hence, don't try to imitate every wide curve or jerky "drop ball" you see, if, after a trial, you find it leaves your arm aching and sore. And above all things, don't worship at the shrine of that finger magic which makes a ball do strange tricks in the air, at the expense of control. Any big League pitcher will tell you that no matter what curves, jumping balls, and deceptive deliveries you may have, your prowess goes for naught if you lack that one thing—control. If you can "put it where you want it," and have not even a suspicion of a curve, you can pitch a better game and "hold down," the opposing batsmen more effectively, than can the finest curve and jump ball pitcher ever born who can *not* make his curves break over the plate, and whose jump ball always misses the corners.

Batsmen are a canny lot. They don't reach after wide ones when wide ones come toward them constantly. Making the batter "bite" at a bad ball—one which is not over the plate—is half the art of pitching, and that art centers in the ability to control the ball. Almost any good pitcher can pitch a "strike" eight times out of ten—if he really wishes to do it. But he doesn't. Most of them want to throw just enough strikes to fool the batsmen, and pitch balls which the batter will hit at and either "pop up" or "foul off" or knock down for an easy play. If he has not control, the pitcher will issue passes, hit batsmen, and put balls over the plate just when he *wants* to keep them away, and then the opposing batsmen will "slaughter" him.

How a pitcher, by losing control, may "break up" a defensive play, was shown in a game between the Cleveland and Chicago clubs of the American League. The late Addie Joss, of Cleveland, was pitching. There was a man on first and one on second, and only one out. Joss was signaled for a waist-high ball, close in to the batter, yet over the plate, because the natural play was a bunt, and Cleveland wanted to frustrate it; and such a ball is hard to bunt. Sullivan, catcher of the Chicagos, at bat, will probably hit such a ball near second base, if he hits it at all. With the pitch, Lajoie, the Cleveland second baseman, started for the logical place to field the ball, if Sullivan hit it. But Joss's hand slipped, the ball went low, cut the heart of the plate, and was bunted half-way between first and second. Joss was unable to reach the ball, the Cleveland first baseman had run to the bag to get the ball in case Lajoie fielded it, for a double play, Lajoie couldn't get to the *bunt* in time to make a play because caught going in the wrong direction, and all three runners were safe. Two runs eventually scored. Had Joss had control of the ball, all this wouldn't have happened.

So it is good advice to take—practise, practise, practise, you lads who would be pitchers, but practise for *control*, first! Learn to put the ball where you want it with an easy, firm motion, and without any curve at all, save the natural curve. Once you have control of your straight ball, so that you can send one over the left corner, one over the right corner, and the third over the center of the plate, to your catcher's orders, twice running, you can commence on your curves and "break" deliveries. But practise these gently. *Don't* try to see how wide a curve you can throw, or how big a "jump" you can get on the ball—see how wide a curve and how much a jump you can get on it *with control*. A ball which curves and doesn't go where you intend it, is worse than useless to you. If you can't curve them but an inch or two without losing control, don't use that curve.

Another word of caution: don't pitch without warming up. Big League pitchers don't warm up for fun—they do it because they know they will hurt their arms if they don't. Warm up ten minutes before the game, pitching easily at first, then harder and harder, until you are "burning them through," but, just because you are a boy, don't neglect that warming of the arm and limbering of the muscles that regular pitchers have found essential before taking their places in the big League games. (See Chapter VIII.)

When you see half a dozen pitchers warming up before a game, and one is finally selected, and the others, including Mathewson, or Walsh, or Bender, or Ford, are sent to the bench, what does it mean? It means that all six of the men who have warmed up were possibilities, but that the one selected showed the most "stuff on the ball," as the expression is, and, at the same time, the best control. On the rare occasions in which men like Mathewson, of the "Giants," Brown, of the "Cubs," Johnson, of the Washington Nationals, Bender, of the Athletics, or Ford, of the "Highlanders," are driven from the pitcher's mound, hammered for hit after hit, investigation usually shows that, temporarily, they have lost control of the ball. It may be an unexpected breeze striking the ball, or a muscle "kink" in the arm, or it may be a mental cause, entirely, but it is almost always the loss of control of the ball, and not loss of strength or ability to make the ball curve or jump, which makes a pitcher lose a game or be hit so hard he is taken out.

And when it comes to the "inside game," the spirit and essence of defensive base-ball, control by the pitcher is everything. Knowing a batter, his weakness, his strength, his character, his possibilities, and a pitcher can tell, within a reasonable degree of accuracy, what he is likely to do with a given pitched ball. In one of the World's Championship games of 1908, between Chicago and Detroit, "Three-fingered" Brown gave an exhibition of that brain, fielding ability, and

Mordecai ("Three-Fingered") Brown
Famous pitcher of the Chicago Club, National League

control, possession of which has made him one of the great pitchers of his time. Chicago was two runs to the good, in the fourth inning. But Detroit was fighting, and fighting hard, and somehow Brown slipped a bit, and O'Leary and Crawford each got a single and perched on first and second, with Cobb at the bat.

Naturally, Cobb wanted to bunt. He is a beautiful bunter, and so fast that he turns more bunts into hits than you would well believe, unless you saw him do it. And a bunt, successful, meant the bases full and none out. Such a situation meant a run, two runs, perhaps the game.

Cobb knew he was going to bunt, Brown knew he was going to bunt, O'Leary, on second, knew Cobb would bunt—every one knew Cobb would bunt. "General" Hugh Jennings, of course, figuring that the bunt would be fielded to third base for a force play on O'Leary, "expected every man to do his duty," which, translated into base-ball, meant that he expected that O'Leary would take a big lead and run and slide, that Cobb would bunt short toward third and also run and slide, and that Crawford would take second on the play.

But "Three-fingered" Brown looked further ahead. He walked

to Steinfeldt, the third baseman of the "Cubs," and told him:

"Keep to the bag. The ball is coming to you, and coming hard—watch!"

Kling, catching, signaled Brown for a fast ball, over the inside of the plate. But Brown demurred. He had his own plan. He let Kling know he would pitch a curve, low, to the outside corner of the plate. It was the ball of all others Cobb wanted most. Brown knew he wanted it, and planned to let him bunt, just as he wanted to, but Brown knew his three fingers and his arm and looked further ahead than Cobb, for the Chicago twirler is a master strategist.

Johnny Evers
Second baseman of the Chicago Cubs

Brown pitched. The ball went exactly to the spot he had intended it should. Cobb made a beautiful bunt toward third base. O'Leary was half-way to third by the time the ball struck the bat. It looked as if the play had succeeded. But, starting with his pitch, Brown had run to the third base foul line. He met the ball as it rolled, picked it up on the run, whirled, and without looking, threw it with all his strength straight into Steinfeldt's hands. O'Leary was forced out by yards. The crowd went crazy, and Detroit, puzzled and sore, "blew up," and two more brilliant plays retired the side.

As an example of pitching brains, that feat stands supreme. As an example of the importance of control, it is good to read over a second time—for had Brown not been able to put the ball *just* where he wanted it, Cobb could not have made the bunt *just* where Brown wanted him to make it. And as an example of the importance of the pitcher as a fielder, it is worthy of emulation by any boy, particularly by the boy who has the exaggerated idea of the pitcher's importance so firmly fixed in his head that he thinks only of base-ball in terms of curves and shoots, and never of the pitcher as a batter or as a fielder.

Pitchers are of all kinds, but the most successful are those who can "pitch with their heads," as well as with their hands and arms. Pitchers usually follow the catcher's signals, in delivering balls, pitching to the best of their ability what he orders. Sometimes, as in the last incident, the pitcher will signal the catcher what he will pitch, and so a code should be arranged between the two, by which the pitcher can indicate if he approves of the signal and will follow it, or if he wishes to change it. No good pitcher ever "crosses" his catcher, that is, accepts a signal and then pitches some other kind of ball, for to do so may mean that the catcher, "set" for a low ball to the left, may miss a high one to the right entirely, thus having a "passed ball," and allowing a run to score or a base to be stolen. Moreover, injury to the catcher may result from pitching the kind of ball that he is not expecting.

As a general rule, it is for the catcher to say when a hit shall be allowed, that is, when it is right for the pitcher to "put one over," and allow the batter to hit it. This is often done to save the pitcher's arm, when the game is not at a crucial stage, when the pitcher is tiring, or when there are so many runs to the good that it is right to take chances of fielding the hit, or when a force play seems probable. But sometimes the pitcher will save himself in this way, without the catcher's orders, not by "crossing" his signals, but by letting up in his speed.

"Long Tom" Hughes, of Washington, was for years a hoodoo for the Cleveland club, of the American League, that is, he was almost always able to beat them at will. It is a matter of record that they could make hits off of him, when he chose, but could seldom or never win. And when, as sometimes happened, they had two or three men on bases and none out, and the coacher's cheerful cry of, "Tighten up, Tom," would be wildly echoed from the stands, "Long Tom" would then wind himself into a knot, and strike out three batters in rapid succession, all the better for his short rest, and never in doubt that he could do it, when he was ready. "Tighten up, Tom," was the signal for a groan from the Cleveland bench in many a game, and the cry of delight which went up from the Cleveland club when Hughes was sent to a minor League, was only equaled by their wail of sadness when he returned to Washington. But "Long Tom" lost his "hoodoo" in the minor leagues, and in 1911 Cleveland beat him well and often in sweet revenge for those lean years when he had been their master. Such is base-ball fortune.

As an example of how pitching can de done with brains as much as with the arm, consider little Johnny McGraw, manager of the New York "Giants," as a pitcher. He is not so known to fame, but, perhaps as much for a joke as anything else, he pitched three and two-thirds innings against the Atlanta team, in spring training, in 1911, and allowed one hit. All he pitched was a slow "floater" and a "cross-fire" straight ball, nothing but what any batsman could hit easily—*if* he knew it was coming. But the Atlanta batsmen had been facing Marquard's swift pitching, and the change to McGraw's slow ball and "cross-fire" fooled them completely.

Pitchers should be able not only to throw to the plate with accuracy, but to first, second, and third bases. The laws of the game require a pitcher to take a step and to look toward a base when he throws to catch a man "napping," otherwise the throw is "balk" and the runner may advance. But the good pitchers learn to throw to bases at the same instant they look, and to make the step coincident with their throws—some produce a "near balk," so finely executed that runners dare not take a lead of more than five feet—and the help this is to the catcher in preventing stolen bases, and to the whole play of the defense, in preventing the hit-and-run and sacrifice plays, is incalculable.

Here, as elsewhere, control is necessary—the ball must go straight and true to the baseman, and must be so aimed that it does not conflict with the runner. Throw low, rather than high. Throwing low rather than high forces the fielder's hand down, and he is then ready to touch the runner as he comes in or slides back to the base. But the throw to first should not be so low that it drags the baseman off the bag, or causes him to reach too far forward, as then he is in no position to "put it on" the man coming back to the base. Of course, any throw to the first baseman on the play from a *batted* ball does not have to be low, since then the baseman does not have to touch the runner at all.

If your team of boys are playing together constantly, always have a set of signals between pitcher and the fields, infield and outfield. The infield can usually see the catcher's signals, the outfielders cannot. It is important that the fielders know what to expect. In big League games, you will see the whole field shift for different batters, and sometimes more than once for one batter, indicating that a change has been made in the kind of ball to be served to him. Thus, certain men will hit low balls high in the air, and waist-high balls on the ground. If a low ball is to be pitched, the outfield must know and

A Remarkable Photograph of a Sharp Play at Third Base
The runner just beginning to slide, the umpire running to see the play, the coacher giving the signal to slide

prepare for a fly. The signal to tell them may be a double swing of one arm, a rub of the hands in the dirt—any seemingly natural motion may have an arbitrary meaning attached to it.

A pitcher who has a knowledge of batters is thus better able to play the game than one who has not. This knowledge is usually shared between pitcher and catcher, but the pitcher must not depend too much on his catcher for this information. Often a pitcher finds that some batter supposed to hit a certain delivery easily and to be unable to hit another delivery at all, has "reversed his eye," so that he hits what formerly he was unable to "see," and now cannot hit balls that formerly were easy for him. In case this reversal is sudden, the catcher may call for the ball that the pitcher knows must not be served, and it is in cases of this kind where the pitcher must insist on changing the signal, even if it be necessary to stop the game long enough for him to consult with the catcher. This is often the purpose of those little mid-diamond conversations between pitcher and catcher, when the bleachers roar at the two, "Tell him all about it, now." As often, however, these little interludes come from the catcher's desire to steady the pitcher by a word of caution or encouragement.

There was a newspaper interview printed not long after the 1911 World's Series in which it was claimed that the Philadelphia players were able to tell, by watching "Matty," when that pitcher was going to deliver his famous "fade-away" by an unconscious movement of his foot. This was denied by Matty (of course) but with the very sensible query "where do those who are responsible for this story suppose all the batters of the National League have been looking, not to speak of my manager, McGraw, if all these years I have been making betraying motions with my foot when I was to pitch the 'fade-away'?"

Nevertheless, the incident shows that pitchers must watch most carefully whether or not they betray what they will pitch by their movement and position.

Not only must the pitcher see to it that no motion of his betrays what the pitch is to be—that no unconscious settling in position, turn of the wrist or position of the hand indicate to the hawk-eyed batsman whether to expect a curve, a drop, a straight ball or a "spitter," but the fielders, too, must watch themselves for the same thing. Sullivan, of the White Sox, captain and manager of his team when they were known as the "hitless wonders" from their standing in the League race and ability to make runs by strategy and cunning when they couldn't "connect" with their opponent's pitcher's delivery, watches the short-stop and second baseman, instead of the pitcher. When Sullivan steps to the plate his eyes are fastened on these two fielders. He finds they not infrequently indicate to him, by a change in their position, by the way they poise on their feet, which way they expect the ball to be hit. Knowing this, he can guess what the pitcher will offer him—an out-curve if they expect the ball to right field, an in-curve if they seem to expect it to left. Of course, not all fielders make such movements, and not always, when they do, does the pitcher deliver the ball so that it is hit as it was expected, but the percentage is in favor of the batsman making a hit, if he knows what to expect in the way of a pitched ball, and so, when Sullivan finds a short-stop or second baseman who will unconsciously tell him what to expect he has a "field day" at bat!

That the pitcher must know something of base-ball strategy is easy to understand. For instance, the spectacle of a pitcher passing a man to first base, with two men on and one out, is not unusual, particularly if one of the runners is on third. The idea is this: a man on third, and one on first, means that the man on first will probably steal anyway. If, then, the forthcoming hit, which the defense fears, "goes through" first base, a run will score, even if the ball be fielded, because there is not time to make a play to second or third and to home also. But if all three bases be occupied, there may be a good chance to make a double play and retire the side, without throwing home at all. The good defensive general will sometimes order his pitcher to fill the bases in such circumstances, other things being equal, or the pitcher will do it on his own responsibility, if the man at bat is a heavy hitter and the man following is weak, or if he has been hitting weakly, or not at all, or on the ground. Note, too, that with the bases full, the "double" can be made to *any* two stations, in a force play, with no necessity to touch the runner, a great advantage when speed is necessary.

Connie Mack, the canny Scot leader of the Champion Philadelphia Athletics, has a theory that when a pitcher is being hit hard, it is oftentimes the catcher and not the pitcher who should be changed.

In other words, that a catcher is largely responsible for a pitcher's success or failure.

That this is absolutely true, no pitcher who has ever pitched to a first-class catcher will deny. Let us imagine that you who read this were absolutely perfect in the mechanical work of a catcher—that you could catch the most difficult pitches, throw accurately to all bases, and knew to a hair just where each ball you signaled for from the pitcher would come. But there your knowledge is supposed to stop. You don't know anything at all about batters, or defensive generalship.

You are playing against a team which is composed half of right-hand, half of left-hand batters. Your pitcher is a "speed-ball artist," with a slow drop to "mix in." What will you tell him to pitch? To which batter will you have him pitch the fast ball inside, to which the fast ball outside? To which batter shall he serve slow drops, mixed with wide balls, to which slow drops mixed with fast ones, high, to which fast ones, low, mixed with wide and teasing balls that just fail to be strikes? You don't know. You are bound to guess wrong much of the time. And every time you guess wrong and order the pitcher to give Cobb a waist-high ball over the plate, he knocks it out of the lot. And when you try to fool Magee, of the "Phillies," or Wagner, of Pittsburgh, or Lajoie, of Cleveland, by calling for "teasers" which just fail to be strikes, you find they treat them just as if you held the ball still for them to hit, and knock them out of the lot, too. Is it the pitcher's fault? It is not. It is *your* fault. But put in a great catcher, even one who has less mechanical ability than that you are here supposed to possess. Let it be Thomas of the "Athletics," "Red" Dooin, of the National League "Phillies," Gibson, of Pittsburgh, Street, of Washington, Sweeney, of the New York "Highlanders," and see the difference. The pitcher is called on for those balls which the catcher knows the batsmen don't like. He is called on for wide balls just in time to make possible the throw to second to stop a steal. He is steadied, encouraged, played upon, by the catcher, almost as a musical instrument is played upon by a musician. So well is this partnership recognized, that many a pitcher is always bracketed with a catcher as a great "battery," as Clarkson and Kelly, of Anson's great Chicago team, or Johnson and Street, of Washington, or Young and Criger, formerly of Boston.

So you, as a catcher, must learn to know the opposing batsmen and their weaknesses—and you must also know your pitchers and just what they can and cannot do. It is idle to demand a low drop on the inside of the plate from a pitcher who cannot pitch a drop except he pitches slow—and you must know all this. It is foolish to demand a "jump" ball from a pitcher who is just beginning to develop one. Know your pitcher, and his possibilities, and play these against your knowledge of a batter's weakness and his strength—so will you be a good catcher and one with whom pitchers will want to work.

In studying a new man—one who has not faced the pitcher before, you, as a catcher, must look well, not only to his position at the plate, but to the way he holds his bat. Does he stand close to plate, crowding it? He will have difficulty in hitting an in-curve. Does he "hold his elbows in the small of his back" as ball players call that position in which a batsman stands with chest out, and arms close to the sides? He can hardly connect at all with a low ball. Does he crouch low over the plate and "choke" his bat—i.e., hold it way down from the end? He will have grave difficulty in hitting a high ball hard, etc., etc.

Having looked at the way the new man carries his bat and at the way he stands, "work" him in this way. Have the pitcher "feed" him the balls at the height you think he likes them, but have him make these deliveries go outside his natural hitting reach—in other words, make them "balls." Have him put the strikes over the plate

Catcher on the Alert to Prevent Base-Stealing

at the height the batter likes them least, thus teasing him to hit at bad balls, which will then become strikes without much danger to your side, and to hit at real "strikes" which are so illy placed for him as to cause your side equally little danger of a base hit. For in such reasoning lies the art of the catcher—in his head, judgment and ability to size the batter up—as much as in the cunning of his hand and arm to throw and catch, and it matters not a whit whether you or the pitcher does the signaling, so you both do your looking and your planning before each and every ball that is pitched.

Stone of the St. Louis Team
Being put out at the home plate by Catcher Henry of the Washington Club

The catcher faces the team. He is the only man who sees *all* the other men. Consequently he is in the best position to give signals to all the team, to plan plays, and to execute a general's orders. He must have many signals. Every time the catcher stops and hides his bare hand in his glove, he is telling the pitcher something. His hand clenched may mean "a drop ball." His hand clenched, with thumb out, may mean "a wide one." One finger out may mean "a curve," two fingers out "a slow ball," three fingers out "a fast ball," etc., and the position of the fingers and hand in the glove, whether the ball is to be delivered high, low, or waist-high. The catcher must signal the first baseman if he intends to throw to the base to catch a runner who has taken a lead—his mit suddenly turned palm out and back may be the signal. He will then ask for a "waste ball" or "wide one," and, getting it, will hurl immediately to first base, where the first baseman has come in on a tearing run, the instant the ball is pitched. With a lone runner on first, both he and the baseman "hug the bag" until the ball is pitched, and then both usually dance away, the runner to get a lead, the baseman to get a chance to field the ball—so it frequently plays havoc with the base-runner for the baseman to run unexpectedly *back* to the bag to receive the catcher's throw, which *he* knew was coming, but which was, of course, a complete surprise to the base-runner.

And do not be discouraged if you do not catch them off the bags. This first-base throw is not half as much to catch runners as to keep them from taking too long leads—it is as much the catcher's business as the pitcher's to hold men to the first sack, and the best catcher, other things being equal, is he who does it best.

The catcher must signal the infield at the same time he signals the pitcher—that is, must be sure some man on the infield knows what ball is to be pitched. Usually the third baseman or short-stop will be able to see the signal to the pitcher, and he can transmit his knowledge to the rest of the infield. This is particularly necessary when a "waste ball" is to be pitched, since a "waste ball" means that the catcher expects the runner to steal, and hopes to make a throw to second to catch him. Second baseman or short-stop, then, must know what to expect and signal each other as to who is to take the throw, according to the probabilities of the man at bat making a hit to right or left of second base, in case the ball is hit in spite of its being a "wide one." The good catcher sees that his signals are plain and understood. To get a wide ball, be all ready to throw to second, see the runner stealing, and find no one on second to take the throw, is not only irritating—it's poor base-ball.

The good catcher, however, never throws without hope of success. He doesn't throw if he is a fraction of a second late in getting started. Many a time the stands yell at a catcher for standing still like a "bone head," with the ball "right in his hands," and "that fellow on first just walking down to second!" And this, if you really know the game, is often funny. For there is no "wisdom" more ignorant than that of the ardent "fan" in the stands, who has seen the runner start, the wide ball pitched, but who fails to note that the second baseman, perhaps, slipped a little in a muddy place on the infield as he started to cover. He knows, the catcher knows, the teams know, why the catcher didn't throw—that it was too late, and that the throw which would appease the crowd might "throw the game away" if it went wide or wild. But the "fan" doesn't know, therefore he yells!

The good catcher, like the pitcher, learns to throw low to bases. The difference in time between "putting the ball on the runner," from a throw taken shoulder-high or ankle-high, is often the difference between safe and out. The good catcher throws low to second and a bit to his right of the bag. And that catcher who can throw without taking a step, who can throw "from his ear," with a short, snappy motion of his arm, clips another quarter-second from the time the man at first base has in which to steal, and a quarter-second means nearly *three feet*—ample space in which to catch a runner.

The catcher who knows his business does not lose his temper with either umpire or pitcher. Many a catcher has learned to his cost, that doing so, and showing it by hurling the ball viciously on the ground, to bounce into the pitcher's hands, gives a waiting and alert base-runner a chance to steal second. The delayed steal is not worked against a catcher who never takes his eyes off the base-runner until he has thrown the ball swiftly, but not too hard, to the pitcher. Delayed steals when worked on the catcher's throw to the pitcher are certificates of the negligence of the catcher.

Often the catcher is able to catch a batter's signal and knows that the hit-and-run, the sacrifice, or the sacrifice-fly is to be attempted; more often, his base-ball brains enable him to guess the play. If the pitcher is not "in a hole," that is, if the pitcher has not pitched more balls than strikes, the catcher may easily frustrate the play by calling for a wide ball, or the kind of pitch the batter bunts least easily or from which he is least likely to hit a high fly—usually a high ball. But if the pitcher must "put it over" to save giving a base on balls, and hasn't enough control to permit the catcher to call for a teasing curve or jump ball at this time, then the catcher must signal the field what to expect—a fly, a sacrifice, or a bunt. His signal may be a pat of his knee for an expected fly; a two-handed adjustment of his mask for a bunt; or three blows of his mit by his free hand for an expected hit-and-run—any natural movement here, as elsewhere on the team, may have an arbitrary meaning. But the signals should be, for easy remembering and ready understanding, those signals used by the rest of the team. Thus, if the catcher signals a fly by patting his knee, patting the knee should be the signal used by all for an expected fly; and if the short-stop or second baseman is properly alert, one or the other, or both, will signal the outfield in accordance with the catcher's signal both the pitch and the expected play.

But a catcher has much more to do than all these things. He must learn to block runners at the plate, by getting artistically in their way when they come sliding in; he must learn to touch the sliding runner with the ball in the swiftest possible way; he must learn to throw from any position, almost without looking; to watch base-runners and make throws to third, as well as first and even second, when it is possible to catch the runner off his base; to signal the pitcher when *he* may catch a man off base; to look carefully to the batter to see what kind of a bat he carries and how he holds it, to discover, if possible, his intentions.

So it is easily seen that the catcher is one of the most vital members of the team. On him, more than on any other member, rests the responsibility for defensive generalship, saving always the general on the bench, whose orders and commands the catcher executes as first-lieutenant. And, in choosing a catcher from those boys who can catch well with the big mit, remember that mechanical accuracy, the ability to stop wild pitches, to block runners, and to throw to bases, is necessary for any first-class catcher. But the finest fielding machine in the world would fail as a catcher without brains, quick thinking, and wide-awake alertness.

If you have two candidates for the catcher's position it does not necessarily follow that the best thrower and back stopper makes the best lad to play the position. If you have choice of two, and one is excellent in mechanical work and slow of thought, and the other is quick of wit, but not so good with the glove, it is still the quick witted one who should have first trial.

For wherever mechanical excellence will stop one run, quick thinking and good defensive generalship will stop three. And that is where the big League managers find their troubles—to get perfect mechanical catching machines combined with genuine base-ball brains. It is their brains that have made the reputation of all the great catchers in the history of base-ball—the fame of the Kellys, the Bresnahans, the Dooins, the Gibsons, the Klings, the Archers, the Streets—quite as much, if not more, than their wonderful ability to throw and handle difficult deliveries.

CHAPTER VI

Fielding

What soldiers behind the breastworks, in the forts and trenches, are to the commander of an army, his players, when in the field, are to the base-ball general. On them rests the responsibility of defeating the attack, of meeting the tactics of the opposing general and his soldiers (base-runners), and of cutting short the activities of the offense by retiring the three men necessary to "side out" in the shortest possible time, with the least effort and the utmost certainty.

Even as an army attacked has more than one line of defense—scouts, pickets, outriders, the main body of troops, and the reserves—so has the defensive base-ball army. It has, as its first line of defense, the "battery," the pitcher and catcher, who, together, strive first to put the batter "out" at the plate, and, second, failing this, to frustrate his efforts to get "safe" on first base. For the second line of defense, the general has his infield, and for the third, the outfield—three men in the "far gardens" who do less fielding than the infielders, but whose duties are vitally important.

To choose the position you will play, or to choose the proper position for other lads, if upon you, as general, rests the responsibility, involves considerable judgment and knowledge. To let a boy play a certain position because he likes it, may be good boyhood diplomacy, but mighty poor base-ball. And, once you get the idea that one position is of greater honor than another out of your head and out of the thoughts of your companions, and substitute the belief that all of you, infielders, outfielders, pitchers, and catchers, are but soldiers of the defense, all equal, all working for the common end, and begin to assign players according to their qualifications for the positions they must fill, you will begin to have a real ball team—not merely nine boys playing ball together.

The first baseman, in years gone by, was a sort of extra batsman on the team, a mighty hitter, who was expected to do nothing save bat in runs and catch the majority of the throws sent him, but to field little, if at all. Today, all this is changed. Big League managers still expect a first baseman to be a hitter, but he must also be a star fielder, cover a world of ground, have a cat-like ability to change his position, play with his feet as well as hands, keep his head, and, at the same time, possess height, strength, reach, a "good whip" (or throwing arm), and be as quick as lightning.

Height and reach are cardinal qualifications. Although there are sterling first basemen who are not tall—for instance, Harry Davis, formerly of the Philadelphia Athletics—as a general rule tall men make the best first basemen, on account of ability to reach far to either side, a long distance if front of them, while keeping one foot on the bag, and over their heads, to gather in defective throws. Chance, perhaps the best first baseman of the National League, and Hal Chase, of the New York "Highlanders," a left-handed first baseman who has set a new standard of first-base play, are both tall.

When Hal Chase first loomed upon the base-ball horizon as a first-base player, spectators held their breath to see him retire forty and fifty feet behind first base and towards second, closing up the gap between the bases and scooping up ball after ball, yet always managing either to be on first himself or toss safely to the pitcher

Johnny Kling
Now of the Boston Nationals. When with the Chicago Cubs regarded as perhaps the greatest catcher in either league

covering the bag. When the ball goes to third, short or second, Chase always manages to get back on first in time to receive the throw. Other first basemen get there with time to spare—Chase gets there in time, but doesn't waste any. The result is he plays further from the bag than any other first baseman in the big leagues, covers more ground and cuts off more hits than any other man covering the position.

This matter of being left-handed is a tremendous advantage to a first baseman, because he can throw in the act of turning toward second or third base, while a right-hander must make his stop of the ball, whirl around, and then, with the throw, whirl partially back again, losing a full moment of time.

The second baseman's work is, by some, held to be the easiest of the infield, because he has less need of a strong arm to throw than any other infielder. On the other hand, he must needs be able to throw from any position, particularly underhanded, and with his body twisted into strange positions. Many balls come to the second baseman all too slowly, slow infield grounders which seem to linger on the way while a fleet-footed runner is tearing down the line to first. The second baseman, fielding the ball, must be able to throw the instant he gets his hands on it, without waiting to straighten up, take a step, arrange his position, or make it easy for him to throw. He must throw instantly, accurately, and strongly, from any pose into which stopping the ball has thrown him. He should be a player who is particularly strong on fielding balls which come to his left hand, because the faster he can move to his left the closer he can play to second base without leaving too wide a "groove" between himself and the first baseman.

If there is one thing more than another which a short-stop must possess, it is cat-like activity. He must be instant in his starting to either side, able to range all the way from second to third base, equally skillful in stopping balls hit to either side of him, able to make the "long throw" to first base (that is, from a position deep in the infield, well back from a line connecting second and third bases) with perfect accuracy all the time, and, like the second baseman, able to throw from any position. In choosing a lad for this position from among those who are candidates, pick him who is quickest on his feet, combined with agility to field with either hand, from either side of his position. If, in addition, you have the services of a player who is calm and cool under excitement, able to think quickly and act as quickly on his thinking, who adds to a strong arm a real fielder's quickness of eye and especially able in fielding balls on his right hand, you have a likely candidate for real short-stop work. Generally, short-stops are not big men, nearness to the ground and quickness in moving being essentials to the position, but there are, of course, exceptions to this rule. Little Owen Bush, short-stop of the Detroit "Tigers," is at one end of the scale, Hans Wagner, the huge German giant, short-stop of the Pittsburgh "Pirates," is at the other end, and while, of course, there is little comparison between Bush and Wagner when

Catcher Gibson
Of the Pittsburgh Club, National League

hitting and base-running come into consideration, Bush, with his small size and stature, makes up in quickness what Wagner has in height and reach. Yet Wagner, and all big men who play, or have played, short-stop, like Lajoie, now second baseman of the Cleveland team, Jennings, now manager for Detroit, or McBride, of the Washington team, are extraordinarily fast on their feet; otherwise, great size would be more of a handicap than an asset.

Quite outside his ability as a fielder, the short-stop must have skill in blocking the runner off second base, and ability to "put it on" the runner—to touch him with the ball in the minimum of time after making a catch. The fraction of a second saved in doing this by a fine short-stop is often what makes the reputation of a great catcher in stopping steals, since, no matter how perfect the throw down to stop the man who would pilfer second base, if the short-stop, who usually takes the throw, or the second baseman, who sometimes does, fails to make a perfect catch and block and touch, the man is safe. Look at the line-up of any great team which has an especially noted catcher, and see if you do not find in short-stop, or second baseman, or both, stars of the first water—the Chicago "Cubs," when they had both Kling and Archer as catchers, and Joe Tinker and Johnny Evers as short-stop and second baseman, is a good example.

Third base is generally conceded to be the most difficult place on the infield wherein to become a star. Although the short-stop will often have more assists to his credit than the third baseman, those the third baseman gets usually result from brilliant plays. The ball comes "hotter" to the third baseman than to any other fielder, except, at times, in a liner to the pitcher, and his throw is, all things considered, the hardest to make. For the runner, in hitting to first or second, puts the ball ahead of him—he and it are traveling, in a way, in the same direction. But the balls the third baseman handles are going in the reverse direction to the runner—the greater need, therefore, for speed of catch, recovery, and throw, to catch him at first. And, be it noted, the third baseman, throwing to first, must throw as far as the catcher does in stopping the stealing of second base, with much less time in which to make the long throw, and after catching a ball from any position or picking it up from any sort of a bad bound.

There is nothing inherently difficult about handling a hot ball—if you know it is coming. Catchers handle several hundred hot balls in every game. But the third baseman, more than any other infielder, has a variety of chances to handle. He must be on his toes to come in for a tantalizing bunt, and at the same time "set" for a line or "alley" drive. He must have very quick wits, to know what he shall do with the ball when he gets it, and be prepared at all times for the long throw to first or the quick underhand toss to second, or the swift and accurate throw home. With a man on second base, the third baseman's problems become greatly magnified. If the ball is driven at him, will he hold it, to keep the runner on second from coming to third, thus allowing the batter to reach first? Or should he throw to first, retiring the batter and allow the man on second a chance to make third? Or should he throw to second to catch the man who has a long lead? If it is a bunt he is handling, he must know whether third has been covered by the pitcher or short, whether he has a chance for a double play by a quick throw to first and an opportunity himself to get back to third, and must never, never forget the man who may be on third, the possible score, and the chance to retire the side. All these things the third baseman shares with the rest of the team, but on him, who is driven at harder and bunted at more, than any other member of the infield, the burden lies heavy—hence speed and quick wits must not be forgotten in choosing the guardian of the third sack.

Because the third baseman gets his hits so hot, he must know all there is to know about the pitch, the style of batter, and the probabilities of where the hit will go. Because he guards the last station before the home plate from the invading army of base-runners, he must have a thinking machine which runs at top speed. It isn't enough for any good infielder to field the ball and get the batter; most particularly should it be the third baseman's end and aim in life to put out the *leading* runner, or make a double play. Upon him, too, the catcher depends for many throws in, to stop a man stealing home, or coming home on a grounder, and, inasmuch as a man may slide over home plate as much as he will, the sliding, diving base-runner comes there with more force than to any of the bags, so that there is the more necessity for accuracy in the throw. Generally speaking, medium-sized and small men succeed better at third than big men, though here, as elsewhere, there are exceptions. Lord, of the Chicago American League club, is rather tall than short, Devlin, of the "Giants," is certainly not small, but McGraw, now managing the New York "Giants," a noted third baseman in his time, is little and

A Bunt Along the First-Base Line
Pitcher and catcher watching the ball "roll foul"

stocky, and "Kid" Elberfeld, formerly of the New York "Highlanders," and in 1911 of Washington, was a sterling third baseman and the smallest man filling that position in either League.

The only way for any infield to play good ball is to get together, stick together, play together, practise together, work together, talk it over together! It is *team-work* which counts. You *see* the big League men taking ten minutes of practice before a game, but you may know they have hours and hours of it in the mornings, for there never lived a fielder, no matter how finished, who couldn't improve himself in his work with practice.

And remember, too, that practice together counts for nothing if with it is not developed that *esprit de corps* which makes each man the real helper of his fellow, eager to see the other chap "make good" and glad to help him do it. Don't find fault. The boy who makes an error which loses the game feels badly enough. Don't fail to praise—

the lad who spears a hot one with his bare hand and doubles up the man dashing for home, retiring the side and nipping a rally, ought to have some pats on the back from the rest of the team—particularly the rest of the infield. Criticize, by all means, when an error of judgment is made, but forgive the error of play, and criticize, when criticize you must, with a slap on the back and a friendly word. It's worth while—"fighting infields" are those which are in harmony among themselves—infields without spirit are those in which each man plays for himself, and is jealous of every other player.

In nothing is the success of continual practice seen to better advantage than in the making of double plays. Perhaps the majority of these are from short to second, or second to short and then to first, whence the necessity of continual practice on hot grounders by second and short, who must learn to "scoop" the ball up and toss it to the other man, covering the bag, all in one motion. And the second baseman, who will the more often cover the bag on such doubles, must have the speed of light in his turning and throw to second—the "pivot" or center position of a double play makes its success or failure. Every second baseman of note today—Evers, Collins, Lajoie, Delehanty—lands on the bag with the proper foot determined according to the point from which he will get the ball from the shortstop, turns even as he makes the catch from short, and whirls the ball over to first, all with one motion. As, of course, double plays do come from all points, and as first or third is often the "pivot," they too must practise the quick throw, the throw without a step forward, which saves that tiny fraction of a second about which so much fast base-ball is built.

Perhaps the fielding of bunts is as important in infield work as anything the fielders have to do—and here, too, the pitcher becomes a real infielder as well as a human gatling gun for the firing of balls. Every member of the infield must know when a bunt is coming, and play for it, and while, of course, there will be times when the batter will bunt once, and hold his bat as if to bunt again, thus "drawing the infield in," and then "slam it out" for a single, the bunt play is generally recognized, and the infield able to tell, pretty well, that in such situations as a man on first, second, or third and none out; or, a man on third and one out; or, bases full and one out; a bunt is very likely to come rolling tantalizingly over the grass. Similarly, with a weak-fielding pitcher, much bunting will be done, and certain men on the team, particularly left-handed hitters who are very fast on their feet, will often bunt and try to "beat it to first," even without the situation of a man "on" to be advanced at the expense of a sacrifice.

The pitcher's fielding work here is vital. He must be able to run in, field the bunt, and throw to base, and he must keep his head and know whether or not to throw to first or second. If the ball rolls down the first-base foul-line, he must know instinctively and decide on the instant, whether he, or the catcher, or the first baseman, can best field it, and if it is not for him to field, he must cover first base on the run. In fact, the pitcher must cover first base whenever the ball pulls the first baseman well forward or far back, for while wonderful defensive plays, in which the second baseman covers first on infield grounders to first baseman, playing deep, have been devised, it is the pitcher's work, and he should not shirk and should practise, practise, practise, on that sudden run to first and deft catching of the often hurriedly tossed ball.

First, second, short, and third, playing in for a bunt, must remember that they have bags to guard, and, with runners on the paths, should hustle to their bags the instant they see some one else is fielding the bunt, for, be it noted well, there is no use simply *fielding* the ball; it must be fielded and thrown, thrown accurately, thrown in time, and thrown *to some one on a base*, who will catch it in order to make a play. And, if the play is not a force, it must be thrown in time and low enough to enable a man on the base to catch it and tag the runner—if there is no one on base to take the throw, all the fielding in the world won't put the man out.

Fielders, both in and out, must back each other up. Train your team to do this all the time—there is the more necessity in your case than in the big Leagues, for, naturally, a team of lads will make more errors than a team of professional experts, the pick of the country's ball-playing athletes. All major League teams are practised all the time in "backing up." The center-fielder should run up behind short, and in line with the coming ball and second base, when the catcher throws to stop a man stealing, so that if the throw "gets by," it may be retrieved without allowing still another base; second gets behind first when first runs in on a bunt, if he isn't covering second; the pitcher will back up any baseman on throws in from the outfield, and should cover home plate on bunts the catcher goes after, if there is a man on third. The pitcher will also back up the catcher on long throws in from the outfield to home plate. Similarly, in running a man down between third and home, the pitcher must "get in the game," running to the plate as the catcher chases the runner toward third, taking the throw home, running himself up toward third, taking the third baseman's place as he, in turn, chases the runner home toward the now waiting catcher, etc., etc. Pitchers who are lazy in fielding are only half-pitchers, and between an earnest, hustling, hard-working pitcher who is fair in delivery, and an expert who is lazy, most managers would prefer the pitcher with ambition.

Plays in which the pitcher fails to cover the plate are rare, nowadays—the pitchers are too well taught by managers who know the game. But they are not rare in base-ball history. Washington, never much of a factor in the pennant race, but always bobbing up and winning games at the wrong time, according to the ideas of teams which are in the race, once lost a chance on this very play. Kittridge was catching—and Kittridge was a quick thinker. There were runners on first and second and the batter hit to short, who threw to Kittridge, cutting off the runner on third, who happened to be Keeler, from the plate. The man on second, of course, ran to third, and Kittridge chased Keeler back to third. Keeler dodged, expecting Kittridge to throw to the third baseman, when he, Keeler, might sprint for home. But Kittridge, seeing a chance for a double play, jumped past Keeler to get the runner from second, standing "flat-footed" and "waiting for the bag." But the runner was alert and "beat him to it," landing safely on third. So Kittridge whirled and threw to the plate almost without looking, to catch the flying Keeler. And, as he threw, he saw the pitcher interestedly watching the play, the first baseman also a spectator, and heard the ball hit the grand stand. So, of course, the man on third trotted cheerfully home after Keeler, and Kittridge said—well, you can imagine what he *thought*, at least!

Infielders must learn to throw more than one way. In addition to the snap-throw from any position, any infielder must know how to "shoot" the ball when necessary, that is, send it nearly on a line from base to base, but should not shoot when "arching it over," as the higher, more curved throw is called, will do, simply because the harder the throw the greater the chance of error. The pitcher who fields a grounder, almost at his feet, and turns and throws with all his might to a first baseman, is as foolish as he who holds the ball and laughs, because he has plenty of time, and finally slams it in to the waiting baseman's mit. Take your time for a throw, when you have time, and give the fielder the easiest chance possible by throwing easily when you can. To throw hard when you don't have to is taking a chance, be your control what it may, that the ball will get away from you and go wild—which is poor base-ball. And never, never throw if you think it is too late—never throw just to show you can,

A Safe Hit
Batsman reaching first base

or because it seems that the crowd, watching, wants you to. Holding the ball instead of throwing when the throw is sure to be too late, even if but a fraction of a second, is good base-ball, for every throw is potentially a wild one—and a wild throw may "throw away the game."

The question between second baseman and short-stop, of covering second base, is vital. There should be a perfect understanding

Caught at the Plate!
Always an exciting play

between the two as to which will take the catcher's throws. The understanding may well be helped by a signal, or a verbal call. Of course, with batters who hit more often to right field, the second baseman is not so near to the base as short-stop, hence it is then short-stop's business to cover second on a throw to stop a steal. On all balls hit through short-stop or third baseman, especially if short is backing up the third baseman, the second baseman must cover second. Never should both cover it, and one or the other should have the command, so that, if both start for the base on a ball neither is to field, the word of one is final. This is particularly vital when it comes to "stopping up the grooves." Every ball-player knows that a space about two feet wide from each foul line at the bases, a space seven or eight feet wide between first and second baseman, and second baseman and short-stop, and short-stop and third baseman, is a groove down which any fast grounder or line ball is likely to be a safe hit. But, although there is about twenty-five feet—sometimes thirty feet—of infield territory undefended out of a total of one hundred and eighty feet, only about ten in every hundred and eighty fast infield grounders result in hits, in the major league. This is the result of "inside base-ball," in which the infielders, knowing the batter, his probable direction of hit, and the pitch to be "handed" him, leave some of the gaps wide open, and close others up, by shifting their positions. If short-stop and second baseman have not a full and complete understanding of when each is to cover second base and a perfectly working signal, this inside play is impossible, and balls will go safe which should never result in hits.

The necessity of covering second by some one, and that "some one" well understood beforehand, hardly needs illustration. But a game between the "Cubs" and the Brooklyn "Superbas" might have been played to illustrate it. It was in 1908, when every game counted—when it was "Cubs" or "Giants," and every game either played was vital. At this particular time, the score was tied, and Hofman was on second. Bergen, catching for Brooklyn, signed for a "pitch out," hoping to catch Hofman napping. The sign was plain, Hofman saw it, and second base and short-stop saw Hofman saw it. Consequently, they thought Bergen would not throw. But Bergen, getting his pitch out, and seeing Hofman—who is very "foxy"—still had a big lead from second, threw. Brooklyn's short and second baseman stood, "flat-footed," in their tracks. The ball went to center field, and the center-fielder, also somewhat napping, hadn't "backed up" enough to get the ball in time to catch Hofman, who scored. That game tied Chicago with New York for the pennant!

It is vital that all the infielders know the outs, the balls, the strikes, and the coming pitch, otherwise they cannot plan their play ahead. And before every ball pitched, each infielder must make up his mind, from the men "on" and the state of the score, and the balls and strikes, just what he will do with it if it comes his way, and here, again, second and short must work together and know each other's intentions, otherwise their best efforts may be wasted.

Definitions of "inside base-ball" are many. But perhaps the most comprehensive in the fewest words is this: "Getting in motion toward the spot where the ball is coming, before it starts."

If your infield can do that—start moving to the point where the ball is likely to come, before the batter hits it—you have developed much of the science of "inside ball." A player in motion can move ten or twelve feet in the same time another player is starting to move. The only way you can know where the ball is to be hit is by studying the batter, knowing his style of hitting, knowing the pitch, and figuring the result. And "inside ball," to be effective, must be played by the whole team, therefore every one must know the pitch and understand batters, their strength and weaknesses.

The outfield is not so busy a place as the infield, but is equally important. The old idea that "all an outfielder has to do is to catch flies" has disappeared. While fly-catching and ability to hold every ball you can get your hands on, is the foundation of outfield work, it is but a small part of it. The outfielder must get under "impossible balls," and, therefore, must be very fast. He must be a strong and accurate thrower and think with lightning speed; the old instruction given to a new outfielder, "Throw the ball to second base after a single," will no longer serve as the main rule of outfield throws in. True, after a single, the ball belongs at second base, and not elsewhere, unless there is a man on second scooting to third, when it may belong home. If the fly is short and falls a few feet in front of the fielder, who *may* then get the runner at first, if he slows up, the ball belongs at first.

The thinking part of an outfielder's work is as important as the mechanical part, and the mechanical part of throwing—when, to whom, and why—is just as important as the catching of flies, the backing up of infielders and the rest of an outfielder's work.

In all balls batted to the outfield which have to be "chased," there must be perfect understanding of who chases and who relays. An outfield captain, then, should be appointed, and his word be law. There is no time to discuss a play when it is happening. The relay man should get the ball from the "chaser" on a perfect throw, and turning, become a pivot, almost as if he were the pivot man in an infield double play, and throw, probably to the plate, perhaps to third base. If possible, do not throw direct to the plate; that is, if you have time enough, strive to throw the ball so it will strike the catcher's glove on the bound. Otherwise the shock of meeting the throw, its inaccuracy by a foot or more, will make it impossible for him to touch out the sliding runner. Don't throw to the plate if you can't make it in time; throw rather to third to make an "out" on a runner and let the run score. Better one run and an "out" than a run, a spectacular throw, no "out," and a man on third!

First-class outfielders back each other up when possible. Of course, right field does not cut across to help left field catch an easy fly, but center goes to right and left to back up deep catches or forward to help in the relay, if necessary, and if short-stop and second baseman are too busy on bags to take their proper part in relays. No good outfield holds "conventions," the "After you, my dear Alphonse" act, as the bleachers call it, when both center and right or center and left chase madly after a ball, stop within ten feet of each other, and watch each other miss it. Have a rule, or a captain, and obey one or the other—there is no excuse for muffing a ball on which you get your hands, and less for letting a ball drop safe "because I thought *he* was going to take it!"

Most outfields are "sun-fields," hard to play in the afternoon, and very hard on the eyes. "Losing the ball in the sun" is one of the outfielders' troubles. Its cure is practice in the sun-field, the use of the mit to shield the eyes, and a quick and sure judgment of where the ball is going, from your first glimpse of it, without that steady looking at it and the sun at the same time which blinds the eyes in a few seconds. Also, if there be time, try catching a ball while standing sidewise to its line of flight. This allows one to look up, without looking at the sun at the same time,—an outfield "trick" well worth knowing and often of great value.

Perhaps the most vital thing an outfielder has to learn is to "get rid of the ball." You have no use for it, after you have caught it. Some other fielder has urgent need of it. Give it to him. Don't hold it—throw it. Throw it to the

Frank Chance
Captain and Manager of the Chicago Cubs

Tinker—"Always There"
Short-stop of the Chicago Cubs

right place, but throw it, anyway. When you see Cobb, Wheat, or Speaker making a double play from the outfield, you realize what a quick "get-away" is. Men making ready to run on swift throwers like these are always in doubt whether they can beat the throw; many a man has been caught flat-footed, jogging slowly back to base after a fly has been caught by a lively outfielder, because he threw in in a twinkling with speed and accuracy, to the base toward which the runner was returning too slowly.

It is as vital for the outfielder as for any other player to know the strikes, the balls, and the "outs." He, like all other players, must consider the state of the game, the runners on, and decide before each play what he will do with the ball if he gets it. He must know batters and the pitcher's signal from the catcher, if he can get it. Why? Because there are four huge outfield "grooves" where long flies mean singles, two and three baggers, sometimes home runs. The only way three men can cover all the ground of an outfield is by knowing where each batter is likely to hit, and what sort of a hit he is likely to make from any pitched ball, and then to place themselves that they will be in the best position to field that ball. Getting there before the ball is hit is the inside play of the outfield. Watch any good major League outfield, and see it shift for the different batters, angling in and to the left for the right-handed, weak batter, when a slow ball is to be pitched him, hurrying over to the right and 'way back when a noted driver of right-field hits has the pitcher "in a hole" so that next one must be right over. For the certain men who hit almost anything, anywhere—the Wagners, Magees, Cobbs, Lajoies, Speakers, Crawfords, etc., the outfielder must trust to his judgment—he cannot play them as he would men whose style and record prove the direction of most of their hits. But even with such men, knowing what the pitch is to be will help, since any right-handed hitter is more likely to hit a fast pitch, on the outside corner, to right field than to left, a slow pitch to left field than to right, and the reverse if he be a left-handed hitter.

Perhaps the most exciting game of base-ball ever played, all things considered, was that which Chicago and New York, tied for first place at the end of the National League season, as a result of a previous game being given to Chicago because Merkle forgot to touch second base on his hit when what would otherwise have been the winning run came over the plate, played off. New York lost the extra game. Chicago won it with a rally starting with a tremendous drive by Tinker, short-stop of the "Cubs," off Mathewson, the famous pitcher of the "Giants." Mathewson, fearing Tinker, who had been hitting him hard, signaled Seymour, in center, to go back. He believed that if Tinker hit the "fade-away" ball at all, it would result in a long, long fly. Seymour disagreed. He thought a low line fly was probable. But "Matty" was right. He pitched the "fader," Tinker smote it with a mighty swat, and it rose and sailed and sailed—

and underneath it, no one knows what desperation in his heart, raced Seymour, striving to get there as soon as the ball did, realizing that he had disobeyed the signal. But Seymour is human and that ball was inhuman. And it dropped safely, rolling to the surrounding crowd, Tinker making three bases on it. Had Seymour played the "inside game," as "Matty" had given him a chance to do, he would have been where the ball was hit before it started!

Certain outfields play always the "outside distance," that is, as far back as they dare for the farthest-hit balls, depending on speed to allow them to come in for short flies. Others play the "inside distance," figuring that there are more short than very long flies, and that the difficulty of going back for a long fly is less than that of coming in for half a dozen short ones. Other outfields play the middle distance, or shift constantly with different batters. But, of late years, the outfield has been gradually creeping in, since inside ball, better pitching, and a knowledge of batters cut down the number of high, long flies, and better outfielding has enabled men to turn and run with the ball and make "grand stand" catches with one hand. Lajoie, in a moment of disgust after Milan, a remarkably speedy outfielder who plays center field for Washington, had speared what appeared to be a three-base-line fly, high in air, on a dead run to deep left center, remarked:

"Outfielders are not what they used to be. They used to let us hit the fence, once in a while. Now they run three miles, jump fourteen feet in the air, and catch impossible balls at the backs of their necks with their thumbs!"

Plain catching of easy flies is good fun in practice, but little use after the eye and hands are trained. The great fielding outfielders, like Wheat, or Cobb, or Speaker, must learn to "run three miles and catch them on their thumbs!" Practise catching flies which you can't catch! Practise running, for speed is half the outfielder's stock in trade;

practise making the impossible play, and some day you will pull it off. Practise, too, in winds, high and low; learn to figure on the wind and what it will do, for just so surely as you fail to do so, just so surely will a hard-hit drive act against a head wind just as the massed billow of air acts on a fast pitch—cause the ball to "jump" and "shoot," and you will miss the catch which wind practice and judgment would have permitted you to catch, and perhaps with it lose the game.

Spectacular outfield catches are daily features of almost every game. Some are historic. Among them is "Wee Willie" Keeler's famous catch on the slanting fence in right field at Baltimore, in the Oriole days, when Baltimore had a club which was world famous. It was in the fag-end of the season, and Boston and Baltimore were tearing each other to pieces to win the pennant. Stahl, always a terrific hitter, drove a fly to right that looked good for a home run. Keeler, always fast, started after the ball. He ran as long as he could at the base of the fence, which sloped upward at an angle, then turned and ran up the fence. As he neared the top, the ball began to drop—over the fence! But Keeler caught it, ran along the top of the fence for a moment, holding it aloft—then fell over! You can imagine the ovation he received when he returned, limping, but happy!

Chapter VII

Generalship of Defense

"Inside base-ball" reaches its highest development in the defensive game. No one can reduce the matter to figures, but from the difference in the performances between teams of skilled players, and teams with less individual brilliancy but greater practice in working together, it seems fair to say that a good system of "inside base-ball," a "clockwork" infield, and brains in the defensive general, will win, other things being equal, over a team of much better players who depend only on "straight" base-ball for making scores. In other words, a first-class infield defense will nullify hitting and destroy the effectiveness of base-running in a great many circumstances where "straight" base-ball (meaning only the stereotyped plays) would be ineffective.

"Inside" defense requires, generally speaking, quicker thinking and acting and better base-ball brains than "inside" offense, for the simple reason that the offensive general has time to plan ahead, and knows in advance what he is going to do. The defensive general must often wait until the offense is in action before he plans and executes a counter move. Frequently, of course, he outguesses the offense before the play, but as often, an unforeseen strategic move will be set in motion, whereupon his defensive genius is put to the greatest test.

Moreover, the defensive base-ball army must often play first and get orders afterward. When an unexpected double steal is attempted, there is no time to get orders from the bench. It is because of this necessity to play the game at the instant and on the instant, in defense, that team-work, practice, and familiarity with a code of signals are an absolute necessity for good "inside" defensive work.

Never forget this: for every offense, there is a defense; for every plan or act which may result in a base-hit, a stolen base, a run, there is a counter plan, a defensive act, by which the players in the field may nullify the batter's efforts. If, as sometimes happens, the defense and the offense are exactly equal, a tie game results, or a called game with no score. And if the offense was always perfect and the defense always impregnable, then base-ball would cease to be a game, and become simply an exhibition of mechanical perfection.

But just when the offense is in despair because the pitcher and the fielders work so perfectly, a cinder will get in the pitcher's eye, or his arm will tire, or an infielder will stub his toe, and—something happens! Or at exactly the moment when the defense is getting discouraged because, despite all their efforts, a man is "on" and gradually getting around the bases, the pitcher will regain control and strike out two men; or a fast double play will retire the side with the bases full; or some other defensive "stunt" will work, and "inside ball" is again justified. It is things like these that make base-ball the beautiful sport it is; you never know what is going to happen until it has happened!

As has been pointed out, the first line of defense is "the battery"—pitcher and catcher. Their work only begins with the attempt to strike out the batter. "Getting him" on the bases, and in attempting a steal, is almost entirely in the hands of the pitcher and catcher. The pitcher who can hold the base-runner to first base, or "have him going back" toward first base when he pitches, is "playing the game" and preventing a score, perhaps as much as if he had struck out the man in the first place.

Pitchers, therefore, should study how best they can throw to first with the least warning. The rules require the step toward the base, of course, and to make a balk in the hope that the umpire will not see it, is both unfair and unsportsmanlike. But many pitchers have a "balk motion" which is not, under the rules, actually a balk, and which is, therefore, perfectly legitimate and much to be desired.

Perhaps the greatest exponent of the art of "balking without balking" was Kilroy, who, by patiently pitching at a mark on a fence, which stood for first base, while looking at another mark which stood for home plate, finally trained his muscles so that he could throw suddenly and without looking, and hit the mark. He had little skill as a pitcher, at this time, his arm being worn out, but while he passed many men, and his delivery was "hit" often, he managed to "nip" the runner at first so frequently with his "near-balk" that he stopped base-running. His team (Chicago) managed to pull off an astonishing number of double plays whenever Kilroy was pitching, because when he failed to get a runner at first, it was because that runner, at first, "hugged the bag," and so made double plays an easy possibility.

But it is not the holding of men at first, or catching them off it, but at second and third, which calls for the best "inside" play in this particular department. As an illustration of the lengths to which ball-players will go, let us consider a scheme tried and occasionally worked with success, first, so it is said, by the ball team of Yale University, and later by the various League clubs. The idea is based on a psychological experiment, in which two people, after practice, start counting mentally, together, and see how near they can come to the same number in a given interval. The accuracy obtainable is astonishing; any two boys can learn to count, silently, starting together, to ten or twelve, and get to the last number together, with practice of half an hour.

The catcher, seeing the runner on second take a big lead, signals the pitcher and the second baseman—let us suppose by dropping his glove and picking it up. The instant it drops, the pitcher and the second baseman begin to count. The short-stop runs in to the bag, the runner doing likewise, of course. The short-stop backs well away again, and the runner, misled, and seeing the second baseman also well away, takes an even bigger lead than before. At some predetermined number, say seven, the second baseman runs to the bag. The runner, seeing the pitcher making no move to throw, either does not move or moves slowly. But at another number, say nine, predetermined in practice, the pitcher whirls and throws instantly, without waiting to see if any one is on the bag, thus saving that tiny fraction of a second. If the counting has been accurate and the practice good, the ball and the second baseman's hands will connect over the bag

"Chief" Bender
Leading pitcher of the Philadelphia Athletics

accurately, and the runner will, in all probability, be out. That is "inside" ball with a vengeance, but it shows to what minute details the development of the game can be carried.

Catchers will often succeed by a trick of personality. Certain pitchers pitch better to certain catchers than to others—the famous "battery" idea again. Certain catchers can "jolly" a pitcher, by talking to him, encouraging him, blaming him just enough for mistakes, speaking sharply only just enough to get results, flattering him, encouraging him, where a silent catcher may fail. Other pitchers resent this "baby talk," and like to be let alone, save for a quiet word of encouragement. And what is true of men is true of boys, here. The good catcher learns to know his pitchers and their likes, and to steady the "wabblers," encourage the faint-hearted, and praise the competent, thus getting from them the best they have to give.

Connie Mack tells a story of Mike Kelly, "King" Kelly, of the famous battery of Clarkson and Kelly, to show what a catcher can do, as a defensive player, in helping a pitcher to pitch winning ball. It was when the two famous players had been disposed of to Boston, and during a game in which Boston was a run ahead of Washington (in the days when the National League was the only major League). Boston was fighting New York for the pennant, and every game counted. With no one out, Clarkson suddenly lost control of the ball, and, almost before he knew it, the bases were filled—still no one out. Kelly was playing in right field and Ganzel was catching. Kelly came running in from the field and implored his manager, Jimmy Hart, to let him go behind the bat. Hart assented, so Ganzel and Kelly changed places.

Daly was at bat, and two balls had been called by the umpire on Clarkson. But Kelly knew Clarkson and Clarkson knew Kelly, and Kelly, as never a man before him and seldom one since, knew batters. And Kelly "nursed" Clarkson as a nurse watches a sick baby, and—Daly struck out.

The next man at bat tried to fool Clarkson into passing him, but Kelly outguessed him, so that he struck at the wide ones and stood still for the strikes, and he, also, went out on strikes. Hoy was the next man up, and Kelly teased him by calling for slow ones and fast ones, so that he hit one of the latter and popped up a little foul which Kelly neatly caught,—and the side was out, and never threatened thereafter. Three men were held on the bases, while three others of their side were put out, in "one, two, three" order!

There are, of course, a host of defensive plays in which the catcher has a leading part. With a man on third and one on first, and the man on first stealing, the catcher must decide on the instant whether he will throw to second, or third, or pitcher, or short. It will depend on many things: the state of the game, the character of the runner on third, the speed of the base-stealer.

Suppose the man on third is very fast, a junior Cobb or Collins, a player who can think quickly and run like a flash; the chances are he will try to score when the man on first steals second. Therefore, a pitch out is ordered, and the ball sent high and fast back to the short-stop, as the man on first dashes for second. The short-stop runs into the diamond twenty feet, takes this "short throw" and returns it to the catcher, to catch the man coming in from third. But suppose the man on first doesn't go to second. Suppose two pitch outs are made. Then the batter has the pitcher "in a hole." He is probably taking a good "toe hold," expecting the next ball over the plate, and if he hits it, may score two runs for his side. The alert general will order two more pitch outs, perhaps, passing the batter and filling the bases. The great advantage of this move is that it provides a chance for a force play at *any* base—thus, the next batter up *must* hit cleanly. A ball which any infielder can get his hands on will prevent a score, since it can be fielded to any of the three bases, the nearest one, and, by "forcing" the third "out," prevent the run from scoring.

If it is the ninth inning, and the catcher's side is two runs or more ahead, he may let the man on third steal home and catch the man stealing second. If the man on third is a poor base-runner, the catcher may merely "bluff" the throw, and whirl and throw to third base, thus catching the runner between the bases and running him down. Or he may "bluff" the throw and hold it, and, pretending to toss the ball to the pitcher, whip it to short-stop or third baseman, getting the runner on third base by a "delayed throw trick" and catching him so completely by surprise, that he has no time to run at all, but is "out" with a jab of the ball in his ribs before he knows what has happened. And if, on a throw to third, the runner on third gets back to the bag safely, sometimes a quick throw to first or second will "nip" a runner who is too interested in the play at third to watch for his own safety.

The good base-ball general, acting on the defensive, must consider his catcher, his pitcher, the men running, the state of the game, the score, the innings, the batting order, and—and—well, he must consider everything! But as carefully as anything else, he must consider the use of his reserves, and when it is time to throw in fresh strength against the enemy, not only in offense, but in defense. This, of course, involves mostly the changing of pitchers when the one at work is being freely "found" and does not seem to be "right" and to "have little stuff" on the ball. The study of pitchers, and their strengths and weaknesses, is a great part of the defensive general's work in the big League ball, and knowing when to change pitchers has won many a game.

When Fielder Jones managed the Chicago "White Sox" (American League), he was noted for the frequency with which he changed

A Cyclonic Slide
A hard task for the umpire

Just Beating the Ball!

players and pitchers, sent in pinch-hitters, and substituted men on the infield and the outfield as the opposing sides changed pitchers. In one game be used no less than five pitchers, and won it. When the "White Sox" got in a crippled condition and only one pitcher was in real form, Jones frequently used him to pitch an inning, half an inning, several times one ball, and thus "spread" Walsh, his star pitcher, "thin," but so flavored his games with Walsh's fine pitching that he all but won his pennant.

In nothing does the base-ball general show his genius to better advantage than in the devising of a set of signals and the careful, painstaking training of his men to understand them. As has been said, those signals which are merely arbitrary meanings attached to natural movements or words, are usually most esteemed in big Leagues, because easy to change and easy to remember.

Defensive signals are better as they are small in number. They are those the catcher uses to the pitcher, telling him what to pitch, and are, as has been said, variations of the position of the open or closed hand in the big glove; those the catcher uses with the infield to signal when he will throw to a base, from a wide pitched ball—and a good team will need no signal for this, because the infield will catch the signal for a "waster" when it is given the pitcher and know where it is to be thrown by the number of men "on" and where they are; the signals short-stop and second baseman have with each other as to which will take a throw from catcher on a "steal-stopping" play, and the signals from the bench when a play of the offense is detected or guessed. Thus, if the bench general thinks a double steal is to be attempted, he must decide whether he will instruct the catcher or let the catcher handle it; if the former, whether he wants to let a run score to get a sure out; whether he will let the steal be attempted and trust to fielding to cut off the run, or if he will waste a ball and try to stop the steal that way; and so on through all the variations.

He must, therefore, have some signals by which he can indicate his wishes, if he meddles in defensive plays of this kind. Generally speaking, such matters are better left to the catcher, unless the general is a player in the field, when he will be able to signal the catcher with ease because the catcher is facing him. As good a signal code as can be used is probably the combination of a sentence with a name: this, "Play for the runner" means exactly the opposite (play for the batter), while "Play for the runner, Tom," may mean a "waste" ball wanted, and "Play for the runner, Tom; play for the runner," may mean, "Let him hit and play for the easiest out."

The principal signals used by the defense were discussed in the chapter on fielding; defensive signaling is more concerned with getting players in motion toward where the ball is likely to be hit than anything else, and as this depends upon a knowledge of batters and the pitch, it is more a matter between the catcher, pitcher, and infield, and a general understanding, than any special signals outside these from the catcher to the pitcher calling for certain kinds of balls to be delivered.

But defensive signals, if comparatively few in number, must be well understood, or disaster may result.

At least once in a World's Championship game, Bush and Delehanty, short-stop and second baseman of the Detroit "Tigers," started in opposite directions as the ball was pitched, letting it go safe between them—the result of "crossed" signals.

While it is true that much of the defense must be instantaneous, and dependent on what the offense does, there is a certain amount of defensive planning which can be considered before the game. Thus, if the opposing battery is weak on fielding, in the offense you may order a bunting game. In the defense, the converse is true—if you are going against a team noted for fleetness of foot and strength of bunts, put in your best fielding pitcher. If your opponents are fleet of foot and daring of heart on the paths, and run at any excuse or with none at all, turn to that catcher who is sharpest and cleanest in his throwing and headiest in his work against men on the bases, even if he be himself a poor "sticker" and slow on the paths. Choose a left-handed pitcher to stop stealing, rather than a right-hander, other things being equal. In other words, when you are on the offense, find the weakness of your opponents and play to it; when you are on the defensive, find their strength and guard against their using it as much as you may. It is but the work of the general commanding an army in the field, in modified and smaller form. He looks for his enemy's weak spot, the point in his lines which will give way the easiest, and charges that spot; on defense, he looks to his enemy's strongest attack; if it be artillery, he gets his men under cover, if it be a corps of seasoned men who can stand forced marches, he guards against an attack in the rear; if it be sharp-shooters, he deploys deep skirmish-lines to meet them and keep them at a distance, and so on.

Don't imagine for an instant that everything about base-ball has been discovered, tried, or played; don't copy the big Leaguer just because he is a big Leaguer. Invent a play, if you can, and try it. It may well be that it will work, with you, where it might fail, in the big League, because of the difference in size and strength of the players.

There is a little base-ball story, which may be true or may be an invention, but which is perfectly possible, at least. Every lad who plays short-stop knows that the closer the second baseman can play to the bag, the easier his job is, since the less ground he has to cover. The second baseman, of course, can play closer to second base as the first baseman gets farther away from first base. Now, in the old days, first basemen played all the time on the bag. They never thought of playing "deep" and helping the second baseman, and thus helping the second baseman to help the short-stop. It is related of Comisky, the owner of the Chicago "White Sox," that when he was manager of the St. Louis "Browns," and, to the scandal of the rest of the League, developed his pitchers to be fielders, he received his idea from a team of "sand lotters" under sixteen years of age. According to the story, Comisky was taking a walk one afternoon, and stopped to watch two teams of lads playing ball. The first baseman, as was customary then, played near his bag. But just before the pitch, this first baseman ran way back into the deep infield. The batter hit to him sharply, and Comisky turned away, expecting nothing better than that the batter would be safe, since the baseman could not get back in time. But the shrill cries of the small audience made him turn back just in time to see the diminutive pitcher reach first base a step ahead of the runner and receive the ball thrown from the equally diminutive first baseman, thirty feet away. The base-ball world knows that Comisky's St. Louis team revolutionized that part of the defensive game. That a boy's team started the revolution is the tale—at any rate, it is a good story. Incidentally, it may be said that a similar story is told of Callahan, of the "White Sox," and a defensive play to stop a double deal, in which, with men on third and first, the pitcher throws to third and he instantly to second, to catch the trailing, not the leading man, which, so the story goes, Callahan evolved from seeing boys play it that way. But no one really knows.

The most famous inside base-ball defensive play ever made, judging by the furore it created, was that in which Johnny Evers, the second baseman of the Chicago "Cubs," managed to keep his team in the race and finally to win the coveted pennant over New York by a one-game margin, in 1908. Reference is made, of course, to the famous "Merkle incident." It will bear retelling, in a few words, for the sake of the brains that turned Merkle's slip into a pennant for Chicago. In the last half of the ninth inning, with the score one to one, Merkle on first base, McCormick on third base, Bridwell at bat, two out, and the outcome of the game deciding the pennant, practically, the moment was about as tense as any which ever arrived in base-ball. Bridwell hit safely, cleanly, a line hit to center field. McCormick crossed the plate. Bridwell touched first base. The crowd went mad. New York had apparently won, two to one. But Evers, still standing on second, called for the ball, got it, and claimed that Merkle, who had trotted to the clubhouse, *had not touched second base*, and that, as he had legally to leave first base to make place for Bridwell, and had not touched second base before the ball got there, *he was forced out*, and that the run, therefore, did not count. The umpire, O'Day, reserved his decision and suspended play.

The uproar raised is history, but the base-ball commission which sat on the case awarded Chicago the decision, on the rules, and is now generally conceded to have done right. The rule is plain. It reads as follows:

> Rule 59. One run shall be scored every time a base-runner, after having legally touched the first three bases, shall legally touch the home base before three men are put out; provided, however, that if he reach home on or during a play in which the third man be forced out or be put out before reaching first base, a run shall not count. A force out can be made only when a player legally loses the right to the base he occupies, and is thereby obliged to advance as the result of a fair hit ball not caught on the fly.

In the play-off of the resulting tie, Chicago won, because, as has been related, Seymour didn't play deep enough on "Matty's" signal, and Tinker drove a ball over his head.

Now in the rush and roar of the spectacular finish of a vital game, before an immense crowd, it took considerable brains and quick thinking for Evers to figure out that the game really was a tie.

The crowd leaving the old Polo Grounds at the close of a game.

From the beginning of the game, players have left the field with the winning run crossing the plate in the ninth inning. No one really blamed Merkle at all. He followed a custom. Evers followed the rules, and his quick wittedness saved a pennant. It is interesting, though not important, to know that McCormick, now out of baseball, says it was Hofman who "called the turn," though Evers caught the ball on second and did the arguing.

All "inside ball," therefore, is not actual play; much of it is done in quiet hours; some of it, as in this case, in strenuous circumstances but after play has ceased; all of it must be accomplished first, within one's head.

Another instance of "inside" defense which involved more thinking than doing, is related of Connie Mack, who was as great an inside player in his time as he is now a base-ball general. In this instance, he "put one over" on wise old Captain Anson, which Anson never forgave him. Connie was then with Pittsburgh. The Chicagos needed a run to tie, there were two out, the bases filled, and Anson at bat. Anson was the premier hitter of his time, especially with men on the bases, and it looked stormy for Pittsburgh. With the call two and two, Mack ran to Gumbert, pitching, and told him to "waste" a ball, but make it close to the plate, and to pitch the next ball, which had to be a strike, *instantly* on the signal. Gumbert obeyed, and the curve slid over eight inches to one side of the plate.

"Good strike, that," said Connie Mack, tearing off his mask and starting for the bench.

"Strike? Strike?" cried Anson. "You call *that* a strike?" indignantly to the umpire.

"I didn't say so," imperturbably replied the man in blue. "Three balls."

Anson grumbled.

"I should say it wasn't—strike, nothin'!"

But meanwhile Connie Mack had given Gumbert the signal. Mack was not in position to catch, his mask was on the ground, and nothing in his attitude told Anson or the umpire he was expecting a pitch. The ball cut the plate in two. Mack managed to jump in, knock it down, pick it up, and touch Anson. Anson never even took his bat off his shoulder.

"Three strikes—side out," said the umpire.

Anson protested loudly for minutes, but the canny Scotch fox had outwitted him. It was inside defensive ball of a kind that was very popular then. True, it wasn't winning by mechanical skill, but any play, no matter whether made with head, or hands, or ball, or argument, which is legal under the rules, and which puts a man out, is good, *professional* base-ball—and this time the trick saved a game.

Chapter VIII

Drill—Battlefield and Arms

The first spring days bring out the balls, the gloves and the bats, and every vacant lot is covered with hordes of boys of all ages, throwing, catching, batting and running, either playing a game or just "pract'sing" for the fun of it.

The major league ball player has been training in some southern clime for weeks before the boys get out, but he hasn't begun as boys always do, and probably always will, begin their ball season. The major league player hasn't been allowed to look at a bat for several days after he starts his spring training, and he has had a disagreeable person called a manager standing over him all the time, exhorting him to "go slow—be easy with that arm—don't you dare throw a curve, you Jenkins, you—Smith, old boy, do you think you are a scow that you try sliding so soon? Jones, if I see you throw across the diamond again for a week, it will cost you ten dollars—" and so on.

Why? Because there is a long playing season in front of these men, and their muscles must be trained and hardened and made used to the strain they must stand—gradually. The morning after the first day's training is an excellent time to be somewhere else than within the limits of a ball park where major leaguers are training, for all are sore and stiff and out of temper. But, had they been allowed to do as they please and throw as hard and as long as they wished, to slide, and bat to their heart's content, they would all have been in bed instead of on the field.

Of course, no one, the writer least of all, expects any boy to pay any attention to this.

"Shucks!" some twelve-year-old reader will say (I can hear him now). "It won't hurt any to bat a little. Why, batting's half the fun!"

And off he goes with his bat and swings until he is sore the first day; and then, later on, he wonders why in the world he can't bat this year as he did last.

No one, certainly not the present scribe, would prescribe as rigorous a training for the lad who plays for fun as for the ball player to whom the game is his work in life. Boys have neither the time, the patience, nor the need for such a system. But any boy who will spend a little time in getting himself in condition to play ball, will play better ball than his companion who jumps wildly into the furious excitement of the game and "plays his arm off," as ball players say, until he is so stiff and sore that he has to desist from playing for several days.

If I were a lad going out in the first spring days for my first ball practice of the year, I wouldn't play a *game of ball* at all. I would get half a dozen of my fellows and form a ring and play ten minutes of "Go to it" or "High-low" (and ten minutes will be found ample). "Go to it" is a very simple "game" which isn't a game at all. It is a lot of fun, a lot of hard work and is absolutely guaranteed to make all the unused muscles which have grown stringy and soft with a winter's disuse, wake up and let you know unmistakably that you possess them.

Boy number one tosses the ball, carelessly, easily, somewhere in the general direction of the lad opposite him. The boy tossed to makes a dive or a spring, or a jump to get the ball, and the *instant* he gets his hands on it, lets it fly in the general direction of some other boy. The whole point is to toss the ball so that some one has to jump for it or stoop for it or move for it, and to throw or toss it the *instant* you catch it. It gets you all in a gale of laughter—which is good for the lungs—and it stretches all the muscles in the body without straining them.

Then, if I were a lad, and really wanted to do a little training, to fit myself for all summer's ball, I would throw the ball for another ten minutes, just easy throws, "arching them over," and then I would run a while and then rest a while; then a little more running and throwing and then—stop. There will be other days.

The point is this—muscles can be made sore to a certain degree without losing elasticity—the next day they will hurt, but the hurt will disappear with more practice. But overdo—practise too hard the first day—and the second day's practice doesn't take the soreness out—it just makes it worse, until every move is a torture.

Remember that it isn't the size and hardness of a muscle which counts—it is the quality. Many a good pitcher has arms almost as smooth and rounded as a woman's, when hanging in repose—but his muscles are long and flexible and the ability is in the body to make every single muscle contribute its quota of speed to the pitched ball. The less attention you pay to the mere size of your muscles and the more to what can be done with them, the better athletic development you will have in the long run.

Not until you have exercised in gradually increasing periods of time for two or three days should you take up your bat. Batting is a matter of quickness of eye and muscular control. It is a sudden, muscle-swelling effort, and to try it at first without some little exercise and conditioning of the muscles is to lose that best of all foundations for a year's good work with the stick, a good start. Wait a few days before batting and then bat only a short while. Get your "whip" (of course you call your throwing arm your "whip," don't you?) into working order, and your lungs so filled and distended with air that you can fly around the diamond at full speed and have breath enough left to speak at the end of your trip—*then* go at your bat.

If you are a pitcher and really have a curve—don't pitch it until you have limbered up your arm well, with several day's work. A boy's arm is less strong than a man's. It is more limber than a man's and gets less stiff, to be sure, but on the other hand it hasn't the vitality a man's arm has, and should therefore receive, if not as concentrated a cuddling and nursing as a major league pitcher devotes to his "salary wing," at least a decent and respectful attention! Whatever you do, don't start in to play by throwing hard and swift balls—no, not even when you are in full condition and in the midst of the season. Elsewhere in this series of papers mention has been made of the "warming up process" which pitchers indulge in before a game—any boy will do well to follow that practice, in the game as well as in his little attempt at spring training, and "warm up his arm" before he uses it.

What is universal practice is usually good practice. In no branch of athletics does a man try to compete "cold." The runner always jogs about a bit to get his blood warm, before running a race. Before any tennis match the contestants indulge in ten minutes knocking the ball back and forth to "get their hands in." The pole vaulter makes two or three low, preliminary leaps before tackling his contest and the crack skater never starts in a race without a dash or two to "get his skates warm." They call it different things, but it all amounts to the same thing—getting the blood to pump swiftly through the veins, and the muscles to limber up. And spring training is only a protracted "warming up" from the long winter's rest.

Professional ball players, all athletes who take their sport at all seriously, pay a good deal of attention to diet and the rules of hygiene.

Of course any one knows that you can't make muscle unless you have muscle building food, and that you can't be strong and agile and do your very best if the vital force in your body is being drained away in other directions. Staying up late at night; over study; too little sleep; too much sleep; insufficient bathing; all militate against athletic prowess.

Don't play too soon after eating. Many a tender stomach gets its ill health from this pernicious practice in early athletic days. And sometimes the results are serious at the time. In the city of Washington, D. C., in 1911, one young man fell dead from acute indigestion, while playing in center field. It was in consequence of too great an anxiety to get on the field and enjoy his favorite sport, without giving the stomach a chance to do its work on the hearty meal just eaten.

Don't play ball if you cannot get up a good healthy perspiration in practice. It shows a weakened condition of the system, and that the body is not in a fit condition to stand the strain of muscular effort. Of course, most boys can perspire with little effort and these cautions will not apply in the vast majority of cases, but they do apply at times, and those times are occasions when neglect of them may cause trouble. Major league players won't play if they cannot "sweat" in practice, and what is good for them, in this particular at least, is good for lads.

By the same token, don't cool off too quickly. Don't drink cold water while playing—don't come in after pitching a hard inning on a hot day and lie on the cool, sweet grass—don't fail to put on a sweater to cool off in, if the day is anything but stifling hot. Your ball playing machine—your body—strong and well made as it is, demands care just as much as any man-made machine, and will work the better and last the longer for such reasonable care as all good athletes take pride in giving to their muscles.

New Polo Grounds. New York
Taken between games of a "double header"

Improper eating is the cause of many a failure to do what one knows one's body, properly treated, can perform. If you "run to fat" and eat fattening foods, your exercise will de divided between strengthening your muscles and taking off the fat. If you eat things which are hard to digest, you take just so much vital force away from your muscles and make it work on your stomach. If you drink or eat stimulating food, you will find your "wind" going back on you. Some boys resent a caution to abjure coffee, tobacco or stimulants as "goody-goody" talk. But entirely apart from any moral question involved, the mere practical common sense of training says that if you stimulate the heart it will be overworked in muscular exercise. Tobacco, coffee and certain foods act as stimulants. Stimulants make the heart beat quicker, stronger, faster for a time, than it does normally. Then comes the reaction when it beats slower and more feebly than normally.

Now "wind," as boys and athletes generally call it, is nothing but a strong heart trained to work. Start running around a track, and do five laps. You are tired, blown, breath all gone, panting, "winded." Why? For two reasons—your heart cannot pump blood fast enough to keep up with the body's demand, under the unusual strain suddenly exerted, and your lungs cannot breathe deeply enough to supply with air the blood that is racing through them.

Run again to-morrow. You do six laps. The next day seven. In a month you may run one, two, three or more miles, easily. Why? The heart has been trained to beat fast and strong enough, and the lungs have increased in size and opened up new cells for air.

"Second wind," about which boys talk much, in making long runs, is but getting used to the suffocating feeling of not enough air, and the ability of the heart to run itself up to an increased pace and maintain that pace while there is demand for it.

Anything which stimulates the heart or contracts the lungs, militates against both wind and "second" wind. Hence the caution against tobacco, coffee and other stimulants if you would bring your body to its fullest capacity to play and play well, the great game.

But training in the early days of spring means more than getting the muscles and the body into proper condition so stand effort without resulting pain and weakness. It means a good start in proper playing methods. The average lad is too anxious to taste anew all the pleasures of the game—he would bat, and catch, and pitch, and run flies, and throw far and hard, and "pick 'em up," and slide, and "run 'em out" and "knock the cover off it" all in the same afternoon.

He is let loose from the captivity in which winter has held him for months and, of course, he wants all the fun at once.

These words of caution, and those of wiser heads into the bargain, to the contrary notwithstanding, he will probably have it; and that is one reason why star boy ball players are just as rare as star men ball players. Any intelligent, average boy, with an average body and enough nerve and courage can become a star boy ball player if he only will. But the will to do it must be strong enough to withstand the temptation to go at it all at once. The lad who spends his first day throwing, and throwing only "soft balls," and throwing them just as straight as he can, his next day catching flies, and his third at the bat, is going to be far more dangerous to the opposition in the first game than his neighbor who has done a little of everything all at once "just for fun" and has had no real practice at anything. This, of course, supposing both boys to have the same natural ability.

But it is hard. Major league ball players in their training always go at things too hard and have to be restrained by their managers—all but the wise old players who have trained before and who recognize the need for slowness, realizing that the ball season is a whole summer long and the race is not always to the hare but frequently to the tortoise.

Take this matter of sliding to bases for instance. Every one wants to slide and slide often and hard. It's part of the fun. But to slide properly requires practice and much careful thought—it also requires a good hard skin and some muscle in the thigh if bruises are to be escaped. Neither the proper slide nor the hard skin nor the muscle on the thigh are to be attained by just flinging one's self at the bag and getting there any way, but by careful consistent practice. This practice should take place at the beginning of the season, and not in the middle of it, when careless habits, timidity due to a hurt in sliding or a poor method, have been fixed by lack of attention to the details of the slide and a persistence in wrong methods merely because "there wasn't any time for practice—we had such a dandy time playing a game!"

What applies to sliding applies to any other operation in a ball game. Practice at the individual acts makes perfect in the playing of the game which combines them all. In a major league "training camp," there are hours spent in running bases, in getting quick starts, in batting, in catching flies, in getting control of the ball, in pitching, in chasing bunts, in doing each and every act that may occur in a game a dozen, a hundred, times over. It is what the spring training is for, just as much as it is to get the physique of the players in good condition. And what is good for the major leaguer is good, in a modified way, for the boy's team. Have a manager or a captain you trust and respect, and agree among yourselves that you will do as he says for a week of training—spend that week in perfecting yourself in the individual work you will be called upon to do in the games you will play and in getting your muscles in condition, and if then you do not lick the team of equal age, weight and size you go against for the first time, which has spent its week in "just fooling around with the ball," why write a letter to the publisher of this book and tell them just what you think of this author!

That boys who play ball should admire and strive to imitate the heroes of the ball field is but natural. That they should endeavor to field, bat and run bases as they see major league players perform these feats, and strive to improve their own play by modeling it upon the work of experts, is laudable. But that they should try to do *everything* a major league player does, merely because he *is* a major league player and without any regard to the difference between his size and theirs, his strength and theirs, his age and theirs, is foolish.

Be his pride in his ability what it may, no boy will, on serious sober thought, declare himself as strong, as speedy, as agile as a major league ball player. But while almost any boy will freely admit this, he will fiercely resent the suggestion that he use anything but the regulation equipment of a big league ball player or that he play upon a smaller field than that which is the standard of the great National game.

Whence it may be believed that the author does not expect this part of this chapter to be popular, since it is, frankly, urging lads, who have yet to reach their full growth and strength, to the use of such arms and equipments as shall fit their size, reach and muscle.

Of all arguments as to good health, the preservation of unstrained muscles, the better physical training which will result from suiting the ball, bat and diamond to the smaller age, size and strength of boys, no capital will be made here. One can hear the scornful:

"Well, I guess I *can* throw a dollar-and-a-quarter ball, and you ought to see me swing that Ty Cobb model bat. I made three hits with it yesterday. And I can catch 'em every time stealing second!"

But it is hoped that the appeal will be more successful if made in the name of and for the sake of the game. Not only will you find it healthy and less straining to use balls, gloves, bats and a diamond adapted to your own size, but you can play better base-ball. You can play better base-ball at once, and you can learn to play a still better game in the future, if you will handle a ball of proper size and weight, and not try to learn the art of hitting with a bat so heavy that you cannot swing it without effort.

If you will get your father to lay his hand, flat, palm up, on a table, and lay your own in the same position beside it, and place in each extended hand a regulation league base-ball, and then have both hands close the fingers around the balls, you will be able to see without further argument that the ball which the large hand holds easily and with a strong grip, is entirely too big for your smaller palm.

If you aspire to pitching honors, you know that the ability to grip the ball very, very tightly adds to the sweep of the curve you can make the ball take. You can see that the small hand cannot grip the large ball as well as the large hand. Why not, therefore, use a ball which is in proportion to your own size of hand, when it is so obvious that you can, with it, pitch better?

The same thing applies to fielded balls. It cannot be shown so graphically on a table with two hands, but it should really need little demonstration that a small hand and a glove that fits it offer less surface for catching, fielding or scooping up a large ball, than if the ball were proportioned to the size of the "cup" of the hands and glove that are to receive it.

That this condition is recognized generally by older men is obvious when consulting a catalogue of base-ball goods, where regular base-balls for boys are listed in various sizes and weights. These balls are not, most emphatically, made for "babies," but for boys—boys who want to play the real game, but to play it in the way best suited to their size.

The same thing applies to the equipment—the gloves, the protectors, the masks, the shin guards, used by young players. There is hardly a boy catcher who will not prefer a mask that fits him to one which is too big and the only recommendation of which is that it is "like the one Gibson uses." But the same boy will demand a regular, man-sized catcher's glove and handicap his catching by a weight too heavy for his arm, when he could do twice as well with a glove which fitted him.

Perhaps in nothing, except the ball itself, is the use of equipment too large for one's size more pernicious than in the bat. The ability to bat well is simple enough in analysis, hard though it is to attain. It is nothing more than the skill required to swing the bat at the right time, and in the right plane, so that it and the pitched ball come together at the right place! Now, the heavier the bat, the harder it is to start it from a position of rest into one of motion. The longer the bat the heavier is the free end to the wrists and arms which hold it, and the more likely is it to "sag" a little under the pitch. If you are batting a larger proportion of high flies than you think properly belong to your batting average, try a lighter and a shorter bat and see if the trouble is not in just this matter of too heavy or too long a bat, selected from the dealer's stock because it is "like the one Eddie Collins uses," or "a regular Lajoie model."

As for the diamond itself, it should be as subject to alteration, according to the size of the players, as the equipment. Yet if there is anything the average boy player is proud of, it is the fact that he plays on a "regulation field." It is a false pride, however. He is merely saying, in effect, to the fathers of base-ball:

"You didn't know what you were about when you laid off a ball field. Why, I, only twelve or fourteen years old, can play perfectly on a regulation diamond—you ought to have made the diamond for big Leaguers a lot bigger!"

For if you think you can throw perfectly from first to third, it is plain that you must think Hal Chase could throw half again as far; if you are confident of your ability as a catcher to stop stealing of second by a rifle shot ball from catcher's box to second base, you must be certain that Street could manage a throw of one hundred and sixty feet instead of one hundred and thirty (approximately).

But whatever your own private beliefs may be, the fact remains that you, a lad, *cannot* throw as far, as strongly, or as well, as a man grown, or, to put it another way, that if you do throw as well, as hard and as strongly as a man grown, you must be greatly straining your arm by the throw which he finds none too easy.

The remedy, of course, lies in a smaller diamond. No, not a "baby diamond," but one contracted enough to make the game interesting—one in which the man on first can't steal second nine times out of ten because you have to "loop the throw" to second owing to your arm "being tired"—one in which every tap through the infield isn't a hit, as it all too frequently is when half-grown lads try to cover a regulation diamond, using a regulation ball.

How *much* smaller shall you make the diamond? It depends, of course, on the average size of the lads playing. In mixed nines, where the ages run from nine to fifteen years, it is hard to settle on any one size as being the best. But there is a scientific way to determine just what the size of the diamond should be, suited to the players who will use it, if you want to go to the trouble. It is this: Have each member of the team circle the bases on a regulation diamond, one after the other, just as fast as he can. Take the time in seconds that each runner requires to go from home to first, second, third and home again. Add all these records up together and divide by the number of players making such records, which will give the *average* base-running time of your team. The average time of a grown man's team may be considered as 17 seconds. The distance around the bases is 360 feet.

Your calculation, and the above statements, give you three sides to an equation, as boys who have gone so far in arithmetic know. Let us suppose that your average time, as a team, about the bases is twenty-two seconds. The equation, the answer to which will be the size of the diamond you should use, is stated thus—22 seconds is to 17 seconds as 360 feet is to xxx feet. Multiplying 360 by 17 gives 6120 and dividing by 22 gives 278 and a fraction as an answer. If the total distance around the bases of the smaller diamond is 278 and a fraction feet, one-fourth of that will be the distance between bases, and this, 69 and a fraction, or say seventy feet between bases, is the size of diamond proportionate to the regular diamond, which should be used by boys whose total time of circling bases averages 22 seconds.

Jack Coombs
Pitcher of the Philadelphia Athletics (American League), "World's Champions" of 1910 and 1911

Seventy feet between bases makes a first class diamond for boys of almost any size to play, and the distance between home and second, not quite ninety-nine feet, makes a much more proportionate throw for boy catchers, than does the "long throw" of 130 feet which so often puzzles a big League catcher (to make it swiftly and accurately), and which is so often beaten by a clever base stealer.

The author is thoroughly well aware that this is not a popular line of argument, that boys are prone to resent the implication that they are not strong enough or big enough to play on a regulation diamond with a regulation bat, a regulation ball, mask, glove, protector and so on. It has not been so very, very long since he was a boy himself who played on a regulation diamond and scorned the smaller ones, just as you who read are perhaps scorning these suggestions! But he wishes to make it thoroughly understood that he is not saying *some* boys are not strong or big or quick enough to play with regulation arms and equipment on a regulation diamond, but that they are not big and strong enough to play *as well* on the regulation diamond, and with the regulation equipment, as they can if they will use the tools, implements and arms suited to their size and strength and fight their battle of base-ball on a field commensurate with both. You play a better game—you have more fun—develop better your ability, when playing with a boy's outfit than with a man's; and you certainly develop your muscles better, and strain them less, under such circumstances than when using balls too heavy and over distances that are too great.

Yes, indeed, you develop your body *better* with exercise which is not heavy than with that which strains it. Lifting heavy weights never produced anything but slow, muscle-bound bodies, often strained ones. Pulling a ten pound pulley weight slowly for five minutes isn't one-tenth as effective as pulling a two pound one briskly for five minutes; playing with dumbbells of iron isn't as good a way to develop arms as if wooden ones are used; running with a weight on one's back will not develop speed. And throwing a heavy ball a long distance, or pitching it to a catcher so far away that the ball must be "looped," will neither teach you to throw or pitch with speed and accuracy nor develop the throwing muscles, as will the same exercise with a lighter ball thrown through a shorter space.

Any boy who doubts this should go, or write, to any great athletic trainer—any man who makes a business of teaching boys athletics—and submit the whole matter to him; and unless the author is greatly mistaken the great trainer is likely to pronounce this, to you the most unpopular chapter in the book, the most valuable within its covers!

Chapter IX

The Rules—League Law

When two nations go to war they do so because friendly agreement is no longer possible and arbitration—the settlement of the question between them by a third party—is not wanted by one of the two. But in spite of the fact that war—the conflict between men of one race and the men of another race, with every deadly weapon science can devise—is a cruel thing, it is not conducted, as was once the case, without any reference to humanity and solely with the idea of doing all the damage possible. There are rules for civilized warfare and they are strictly observed, even by two countries at war with each other. If they didn't observe the rules, other countries would step in and settle the quarrel, just as if you get into a fight with another boy, your companions will let you fight it out, if you "fight fair"; but let one of you use a stick or a stone or "hit below the belt" or "hit him when he's down" and all the rest of the crowd will step in and stop the fight.

Among these rules of civilized warfare are those which prevent the use of poisoned missiles—which produce not only wounds, but great suffering—poisoning a water supply, the use of bullets which flatten in striking, tearing great jagged wounds, as well as those governing the "flag of truce," by which a member of one army can be safe in approaching the other if he bear aloft a white flag, signifying his desire for a conference; the observance of the neutrality of official Red Cross nurses, etc., etc. Recently much agitation about air ships and flying machines and the dropping of bombs has taken place, and there have been many propositions made that all nations agree not to use air ships in war for other than scouting purposes, but so far they have come to nothing.

The point made here is the fact that there are rules of warfare, and that it is absolutely important that not only the general commanding but his rank and file know these rules, if he and they are to fight a winning fight. Let an ignorant soldier shoot at a man holding a flag of truce and he would set the whole world to frowning upon his country. Let a general poison the water supply of his enemies and kill a dozen or more of them and public opinion would so swing to the injured combatant that the war would have to end, then and there. Both the general and his men must know the rules of so-called "civilized warfare," and must obey them.

So it is in the battle of base-ball. Wise heads frame the rules, to cover every possible situation in the game, and every question which may come up for discussion regarding it. This National Baseball Commission is the supreme court of base-ball law, and the rules they agree upon are recognized by all the major leagues, all the minor leagues, all the "bush leagues," all the college and smaller amateur leagues, right down to the smallest nine of the smallest boys playing its first game.

But the base-ball rules are many and complicated—so many, so complicated that there are many, very many, major league players who make no pretense of knowing them all. Not infrequently you see an excited argument on the ball field in which several players are arguing with the umpire about a rule of which until that moment they perhaps had never heard!

There is every excuse for any player's not knowing all the rules—there is no excuse for an umpire's not knowing them all. And while it would be foolish to advise or expect boys to memorize the rules, it is not too much to say that all boys playing base-ball should read over the rules at least twice in a season, and that they should get firmly into their heads some of those rules about which there seems to be, so often, a question or dispute.

You may know how to play base-ball, know when a man is out and when safe, what all the technical terms mean, and just what to do in every situation, and still not know the rules. Major league players who don't know all the rules must nevertheless know how to play the game or they wouldn't be major league players. But any boy who will read over the rules several times a season, will be the better prepared to untangle a knotty point, when it comes up, than if the printed rules are a sealed book to him.

The comments of the spectators at a ball game are often interesting and frequently amusing, when heard by some one who really knows the rules of base-ball.

One man brings a friend and explains the game to him.

"See Evers at the plate? He's going to bunt. Sacrifice bunt, so that man on first can get to second."

Evers bunts—foul.

"Now watch him," says the wise man, "he's going to bunt it, sure, this time."

Evers takes a healthy swing and misses the ball.

"Two strikes. He *can't* bunt it this time, if he does, he's out," says the wise one, and the base-ball players on one side and the trained reporter on the other lift each an eyelid.

"Wonderful!" murmurs the one.

"Stupendous knowledge!" mutters the other and continues to look and listen.

A *few* of the spectators at a league base-ball game

It is, of course, perfectly true that when a man bunts a ball, having two strikes called on him, and that bunt goes foul, he is out. But you will search the rule book for any rule which reads to that effect. What you will find is one sentence in rule 47—"If the attempt to bunt result in a foul not legally caught, a strike shall be called by the umpire." So you see a batter may stand quietly and let two strikes be called upon him and make but one attempt to bunt, which if it goes foul, constitutes a third strike, just as well as if he had bunted three fouls for the three strikes.

That, of course, is just one instance. There are dozens of them. Perhaps the most common lack of knowledge is shown in the matter of errors and of hits. Of course, whether a certain ball should go for a hit, or whether the fielder should be charged with an error, is often a matter of individual judgment. Very frequently it is a matter of individual prejudice. If the scorer is very anxious to see the home team win, he is apt, quite unconsciously, to say that all their advances due to a juggled ball, are earned by hits, and to credit the fielders of the side which has his sympathy with errors when the opposition gets on first or advances on a batted ball, rather than admit that his pitcher is being "found."

But in spite of its being largely a matter of judgment, there are rules to apply, and every boy, whether he score a game or plays in it, should read those rules. In section 4 of rule 85, you will find that a base hit *must* be scored when the batted ball "strikes the ground on or within the foul lines and out of reach of the fielders." This, of course, includes all balls which are plainly out of reach, whether such balls be line flies which strike the ground beyond an outfielder, or "Texas leaguer" balls that go over the infielders' heads and drop short of the outfielders, or balls which take jagged bounds from inequality of the ground, or balls which, while traveling slowly, yet curve out of reach of the fielder.

Every boy knows and understands a hit of this kind.

But let a ball be batted to the left, near the foul line and over the third baseman's head. He runs over, jumps up and knocks the ball down, picks it up from the ground and throws to first but doesn't get the runner. Has the runner made a base hit? Or has the third baseman made an error? While judgment must be used, there is a plainly worded rule about it—"When a fair hit ball is partially or wholly stopped by a fielder in motion, but such player cannot recover himself in time to field the ball to first before the striker reaches that base, or to force out another base runner a hit shall be scored." Note that the rule says "cannot" and not "does not." It is a question of judgment as to whether the fielder "cannot" recover in time to make the throw or simply "does not." If he "cannot," the ball goes as a hit. If it is a plain case of "juggling the ball," or if the fielder's foot slips and he falls down, it may be a case of "does not," in which case the fielder may get an error and the batsman not be credited with a hit. The rule covering errors is lengthy, but that section of it which applies here is short and to the point. Section 8 of rule 85 says: "An error shall be given in the sixth column for each misplay which prolongs the time at bat of the batsman or allows a base runner to make one or more bases when perfect play would have insured his being put out."

A part of section 4 of rule 85 is very important to understand in scoring. It reads: "A base hit shall be scored—when the ball is hit with such force to an infielder or pitcher that he cannot handle it in time to put out the batsman or force out a base-runner. *In case of doubt* over this class of hits *a base hit should be scored* and the fielder exempted from the charge of error. (Italics are the author's.) Note that "cannot" here applies also, but note particularly that "in case of doubt" a base hit "should be scored." In other words, give the batsman the benefit of the doubt, when doubt exists.

Ask yourself how many kinds of strikes there are—that is, when an umpire should call a strike on a batsman. Unless you answer "six kinds" and can name them, you need to read all of Rule 49. And right in this rule you will find the answer to a question which has often puzzled you. You know that a ball which is pitched by the pitcher and which hits a batsman, if he tries to avoid it, entitles him to a base. Yet you have seen a batter declared out on strikes when he was hit with the last strike. Section 5 of rule 49 plainly says that a strike is "a pitched ball, at which the batsman strikes, but misses, and which touches any part of his person."

How many varieties of balks are there for the pitcher to commit? Nine. Can you name them? What are the rules and how many, regarding forfeited games? In how many ways can a batsman be put out? What—*ten*? Can you name them? Did you know that there are six different ways of becoming a base-runner? Did you know that there are seven different ways in which a base-runner may advance a base without being even liable to be put out? Would you be surprised to know that there are sixteen different ways in which a base-runner may be retired, or retire himself, from play?

Well, then, you see there is reason for study of the rules. All these things belong to the game. No, there is nothing to be learned by heart, any more than you know how to play base-ball by any set words or rote. But the sense of the rules ought certainly to be known by all the players—certainly by the captain. The captain is the man who should talk to the umpire, and who should know whether the umpire is deciding correctly according to questions of law. For while there can be no appeal from an umpire's decisions as to a question of fact—that is, if the umpire says you are "out" because some one touched you with the ball, and you know he missed you by an inch, you are "out," no matter what your protest—there is always an appeal to be taken from an umpire's decision on a question of law. Thus, in a big League, if an umpire misinterprets the rules, or fails to know them, and thus makes an error, his decision can be appealed to the president of the league. In a boy's game, where there is no league, the umpire's decision on a question of law should be appealed to a committee of three—the captains of the two nines and a disinterested third, chosen by the umpire, and these three should decide—according to the rules. But unless you, as captain, *know* the rules, you cannot expect to catch an ignorant umpire. And because there are so many rules, and so many ramifications of each rule—sixteen ways to retire a base-runner, for instance—you cannot expect to learn them in five minutes. You must read and reread them, and study them with patience. For base-ball, like everything else, of worth playing at all is worth playing well; and without knowledge of the rules, this cannot be done. So these instances of what the average person doesn't know about the rules have been set forth here at some length, and simplified rules are included in the appendix in the hope that young readers will forgive the "sermonizing" that they should be carefully studied—for the sake of the benefit to the individual player and the whole nine that will surely come from an earnest following of that advice.

The simplified rules of base-ball, easier to understand than the official rules, are reprinted as an appendix by the courtesy of the American Sports Publishing Co. These simplified rules were written by Mr. A. G. Spalding, whose name is known to every man and boy who ever touched a base-ball or engaged in any kind of athletics. A study of them will bring out many points concealed in the technical language of the rules proper, and they are, therefore, particularly recommended to the reader's attention.

In any large body of soldiers, whether it be a division, a corps or an army, organization is as essential as discipline in the ranks, and is distinct from that discipline. A general commands, his subordinates transmit his commands, and in the end, the individual soldier obeys. That is discipline. But in addition, there is organization; the division of responsibility so that one man and those under him looks after the commissary, another the ammunition, a third the engineering features of the campaign, and so on. No individual soldier expects to disobey his captain on the battlefield, for he is well disciplined and taught to obey. Neither would he expect to have any voice in saying in which division of a soldier's work he should be placed.

Professional base-ball players have somewhat the same experience to undergo in their submission to base-ball "law," which is not really legal at all, but which, in its code and its administration, governs the sport from the professional side, absolutely and with no appeal.

Ty Cobb's Quickness
He has just bunted and is already well started for first base before the catcher has lowered his hands

The interest of this side of the game can be to boys who play for the love of it, only theoretical, since they are not, and cannot be, bound to play for the team of which they may be members by anything stronger than desire and willingness to serve their friends and their own love of the game. Yet there is not a boy who plays the game, old enough to read, who doesn't want to look at the scores in the evening paper, and read of the doings of the diamond heroes whose prowess he tries to emulate; and as he must frequently meet with

"Fighting for it!"

the expressions "He was sold for $1,500"; "Jones was traded for Moriarty and a cash bonus"; "The Club drafted five but was only awarded two"; "He was given his unconditional release," etc., etc., a few words of explanation of what these terms mean and of the code of laws or National Agreement on which Organized Professional Base-ball is based, may not be without interest even to lads whose nearest connection to those paid for playing base-ball is a seat in a major league park.

The whole foundation of the system of professional base-ball as played today is what is known as the "reserve clause" in the contract which players sign. By this clause they are "held in reserve" *perpetually,* to the club they first sign with, even if the contract, which may be for a stipulated sum of money per annum, expires. This "reserve clause" prevents a player who is not satisfied with his salary, or the treatment he receives, from "jumping" to some other club. It is apparent on the face of it that without some such saving clause in contracts, the clubs with the most money would always have the most powerful teams, since they would be able to lure away all the remarkably fine players of other clubs. As this would take all the interest out of a pennant race, and make the sport of base-ball merely a competition between base-ball-club owners, as to which had the longest and strongest purse, and would utterly destroy the game as far as popular interest goes, the "reserve clause" may be considered a necessary evil, although players themselves, who have devoted much time to the subject, believe that a long-term contract, say of five years, would serve the same purpose.

However that may be, it is the "reserve clause" on which base-ball in the professional leagues is built, and it is the "reserve clause" which prevents the sale of players without the consent of the management. There are seven other major league clubs besides Detroit, in the American League, and the poorest of them would probably be glad to pay twenty thousand dollars for the services of the matchless Tyrus Ramond Cobb (of Detroit), and some of the more wealthy clubs would undoubtedly bid much higher—how high can never be known until Detroit gets through with Cobb, which will never happen while he can score from the plate on a scratch hit, as he has been known to do, by daring, crazy base running—or while he can lead both leagues at the bat.

The case of "Jimmy" Callahan, now managing the Chicago White Stockings, is in point. He could not agree with his club management and stopped playing. He could play nowhere else—the "reserve clause" forbade, and held him to the club by an iron band. Yet Callahan was a star performer, and would have brought an enormous sum in the market, had the club management wished to sell him. They preferred to let him stay idle, until either he or they had a change of heart, and they could patch up their differences. It was likewise with John Kling, once a star catcher for the Chicago "Cubs." Kling had a disagreement with the club and retired from base-ball. He wanted to play, but wouldn't, under the terms offered him. So he stopped playing. He could play nowhere else; the reserve clause held him! He is now back in organized ball, but figured in a trade in 1911. He found, unfortunately for him, that his "lay off" had not increased his speed and cunning—in fact, that the once great catcher was no longer the star he had been. In such cases, the reserve clause undoubtedly works a hardship on the players, who feel forced to stop playing because they cannot accept the terms offered them. And yet, without that clause, it is easy to see what a hodge-podge organized ball would become.

"Why don't they *buy* some players? says the disgruntled fan, who has just witnessed his pet home club pushed from sixth to seventh place in the league race. "They make lots of money—why don't they spend some?"

But it isn't a question of spending money. In the old days, before base-ball was the business it is now, clubs sold players for the temporary profit of getting a good sum, thinking, perhaps, that there were plenty more players to be had. But now there are not nearly enough players to go round, and managers hang about league meetings, dangling thousands of dollars in their fingers, figuratively speaking, ready to spend it for a Wagner, a Cobb, a Speaker, a Clarke, a Magee—but can find no club willing to part with such a star.

As for the player, he has nothing to say. If he is sold, he plays with the club he was sold to. If he refuses, that is his privilege, but no other club will dare to employ him, since all the base-ball leagues, save a very few, small, weak organizations known as outlaw leagues, operate under the ironclad agreement, by which a player belongs to the club which holds his contract. Of course, a player getting, say five thousand dollars a year, and bought by a club which then offered him fifteen hundred dollars a year, could not only refuse to play under the contract offered him, but could appeal to the National Commission, which in such a case (unless the player was being disciplined for grave misconduct) would probably say that an equitable salary adjustment must be made or the sale would not be valid. And, of course, the last thing the commission or the clubs wish to do is to force the retirement of a good player. In this way, clubs frequently consult the wishes of their players when their service has been long enough to entitle them to that consideration, before selling or trading them. Sometimes marked consideration is shown. Cyrus Denton Young, the dean of all great pitchers, the "Grand Old Man" of base-ball today, was given his unconditional release in 1911 by the Cleveland Club, which reasoned that it wouldn't do to sell, trade or dispose of so prominent and popular a figure as "Old Cy." He then could retire or sign anew, at his pleasure, and at the present writing he (playing with Boston) had just shut out a couple of teams, so it would seem that he is still far from what is popularly known as the "has-been" class of base-ball stars.

Players are secured in more ways than by purchase, however. They may be traded from one club to another, in the same league, either for one or more players or for a player and a cash bonus. They cannot be either traded or sold to any club outside the league to which the club owning them belongs, unless "waivers" are secured from all the other clubs in that league. That is, if McGraw wanted to sell Mathewson to some team in the American League, he would first have to secure the consent or "waiver" of the seven other clubs in the National League before he could do so.

But a minor league may sell to a league club of a class higher than its own, always providing some other club has not a "string" on the player, a "string" being a previous agreement to buy, or trade for, this player. Sometimes several clubs will claim the same player, and then the question is put up to the National Commission for settlement, its word being absolutely final and without appeal.

In addition to buying and selling and trading, there is what is known as the "draft." The various base-ball clubs have divided themselves into leagues, each of which has its own president and each of which runs its own pennant race. These leagues are graded—that is, they belong to different classes—and the value per head of the players is fixed in each class. During a certain period each year, called the drafting period, leagues of one class can draft players, to a certain fixed number, from leagues in the class or classes below them, and, if awarded the player, can secure him by paying the fixed charge for players in that class. Of course, if a player in a minor league shows promise, several clubs in classes above that minor league may want that player and put in drafts for him. In such a case, the matter is decided by lot, the player being awarded to the club which draws him in this way.

It will occur to any thoughtful lad that if the club fixes the salary and then has perpetual right to the services of the player, there is no reason why the club shouldn't reduce the salary of the player as soon as the initial contract has expired. But as a matter of fact the player, mere chattel that he is in many ways, has a very potent weapon in his hands to fight injustice in the matter of salary. The player is the man on whom the club depends to win games. The club ownership cannot afford not to have good players—cannot afford not to win games, because the public as a rule will not support—that is, will not continue to pay to see—poor teams, listless or ill-played ball, or teams which loaf.

Managements are compelled to be fair to players in the matter of salaries, otherwise they fear the players will not play as well as they can—not that it is feared the player will deliberately "throw" a game, but that, his heart not being in his work, he will simply "fall down." And as a general rule, it can be said that although there is a supposedly ironclad agreement by which each club in a league binds itself not to pay more than a certain salary, every club in the league violates this agreement and does pay more than the limit to its "star" players, at its own sweet will and pleasure.

It is seldom that the larger salaries are definitely known by the public. It is to the interest of player, management and club alike that there shall be some little mystery about the matter. It is generally supposed that Mathewson of the New York Giants and Hans Wagner of the Pittsburgh Pirates receive ten thousand dollars—perhaps more,—for each playing season. "Ty" Cobb is reported to get above nine thousand dollars a year; Ed Walsh of the Chicago American League team is supposed to figure in the same class; and Walter Johnson of the Washington American League team is under a three-year contract, calling, so it is said, for more than seven thousand dollars a year. From these figures, the salaries grade down through the major leagues to the minor leagues until they become mere nominal sums in the "bush" leagues, which, with small attendance and not overly good players can afford but little in the matter of salary.

While a salary of eight or ten thousand dollars a year may seem large even to business men, who should understand that such prices are not paid without there being a reason for them, it must not be forgotten that the men who receive these salaries are picked from thousands, and that they are men who make possible the winning of immense sums of money for their club owners. Thus, Ty Cobb has been largely responsible for his team's winning three pennants in the American League—Mathewson and Marquard of the Giants practically pitched the Giants to victory in their league in 1911. Wagner and his terrific clouting, as well as his marvelous fielding and

"Chief" Meyers
The great catcher of the New York Giants

"Rube" Marquard
The Giants' best left-handed pitcher or "south paw"

base running, has largely helped to keep the Pirates in the race for years. And the Athletics' star team could hardly have become world champions without their fine pitching staff.

Moreover, men who receive such salaries, even though it be but for six months' work, cannot lie around and have a good time the rest of the year. They must keep in the finest of physical trim, and report in the spring in good form, otherwise their value would be lost. Again, men of that type and stamp are usually men of brains, whose base-ball success is as much a matter of knowledge, thought, planning and quick thinking as it is of physical ability.

There are runners in the business as fast as Cobb—but never such a base-runner! There are batters who hit *some* pitchers "all over the lot," but very few like Lajoie, Wagner, Jackson, Cobb, Speaker, and Magee, who hit them all about alike. There are plenty of fine pitchers in base-ball, but only one Mathewson, one Walsh, one Walter Johnson, because these men, and the rest of the honor roll of pitchers, pitch with their heads as well as with their arms. In 1910 Johnson held the league—in fact the base-ball—strikeout record for the season, and yet had a lower percentage than in 1911, when he didn't strike out nearly so many men. In 1910 he used his arm, his marvelous strength and speed and cunning of muscle alone—in 1911 he had learned to use his head as well—to save his arm, and "let 'em hit," when there was no one on the bases and to "tighten up" and use his strike-out power when in a pinch.

With it all, men of this stamp must have an abundance of what is known as "nerve"—they must pitch or play better when behind than when ahead. Let the Giants get a one run lead in the eighth inning, and the pitcher falter and fill the bases—out he comes and in goes "Big Six." "Big Six" may not even be warm, but he is perfectly collected. He knows what he has to do and he does it. His team mates play perfect ball behind him—they know that if it is within human nerve and human ability to get out of the hole, "Matty" will do it for them. And nine times out of ten, "Matty" does.

Instances are numerous—but one will suffice. It was a game between New York and the Chicago "Cubs." Crandall was pitching and had held his enemies safe, New York being four runs to the good, when "Big Six," who had kept himself warmed up to relieve Crandall should he "wobble," was finally allowed to go to the club house and dress.

"Matty" got out of his clothes, and into a shower bath, and was having a leisurely rub down, when a hurried word came from McGraw. Crandall *had* "wobbled," two runs had been made by the Cubs and there was a man on first.

"Matty" stripped again and hurried into his base-ball clothes. Meanwhile there was a wordy argument going on between McGraw and the umpire, the latter wanting the game to go on, and McGraw wanting to waste time, to give Matty time to get his clothes on. Finally another pitcher was sent in the box with instructions to be as slow as he could. He finally had to pitch and, not being warmed up, the ball was slashed across the grass to the outfield and now there was but one run needed to tie the score.

Meanwhile "Matty" was having a desperate hunt for his base-ball trousers! Finally they were found, and, running half dressed across the field, shoes untied, shirt awry, "Matty" stepped into the box. Cold as his arm was (cold meaning not "warmed up," or not "limbered up with ten minutes' pitching"), having his whole body cooled with the bath, and taken suddenly from the "let down" mental feeling of a day's work done, and instantly forced into an important game at a critical period, "Matty" had to face a situation which would have daunted many a fine player. But he was perfectly cool, and perfectly confident, dropped three twisting, snaky, uncanny, crawly "faders" (as he calls his peculiar delivery) over the plate, the man at bat took three healthy, desperate, muscular swings at the atmosphere, and—New York won the game.

That is the kind of a man who is worth ten thousand dollars a year to his club, not only from his magnificent physical ability, muscular strength and skill with his fingers and arm, but from his superb control of himself, his skill and his delivery in moments of danger and with the tide turning against him.

And that is why this story has been told here, to meet the objection which many a father will raise when his son comes to him with the tale of the salaries paid that "he isn't worth it." He *is* worth it, this player who stars for his team, whether his name be Mathewson or any one of a dozen or more great players. Like any other profession, brains as well as equipment tell in the long run, and it is the brains as well as the muscle, now being used in base-ball, which make the game one of such great science, and which have raised it in the estimation of all thinking people to the respectability it now enjoys.

Chapter X

Umpiring and Fair Play

When some nation not concerned in a war steps in and settles the matter because one or both belligerents has broken some of the laws of civilized warfare, the self-appointed "arbitrator" is able to effect a settlement because it has the power—a large navy, an organized army, or the ability to get other nations to help.

Base-ball teams have to have umpires, and umpires have to have power. And the lad who holds sufficiently the confidence of his mates to be selected as an umpire can well feel proud that his character, knowledge of the game and fairness have won so signal a recognition. But let the lad who umpires for the first time remember that although it is fine to have a giant's power, it is ill to use it like a giant, to paraphrase a quotation. While there should be no question of tempering justice with mercy or equalizing decisions and mistakes, the lad who umpires a ball game must remember that he is given power only to enforce fair and square decisions, and that it should matter not one whit to him what the rest of the fellows think of his decisions, or what the spectators think of them, so long as he, himself, knows them to have been right.

Does this, too, sound like preaching? It isn't, at all. There isn't a big League umpire who doesn't mind, in his heart of hearts, the

Lajoie of Cleveland

Collins of Philadelphia

The American League's Two Greatest Second Basemen

accusations of "Robber! Thief! Bone Head!" hurled at him from angry spectators, although he minds an ordinarily square-minded player's ill opinion much more. Umpires in big leagues are just as human as any one else, and they must sometimes make mistakes. And that makes them feel badly, too, but no worse than a big League player feels when he makes an avoidable error, either of play or judgment. The player merely makes up his mind he will do better next time, and that is what the umpire does, too, if he is a good one. It is because he has another opportunity that his resolution is the harder to make.

Suppose you, as an umpire, call a fourth ball, and, just an instant too late, decide it should have been a strike. The pitcher is sore, the catcher is mad, the infield is ready to bite your head off, and only the batter is happy. You are very unhappy, indeed, because you want to play fair with the teams and you realize you have made a mistake. So the next man at the bat you call out on doubtful strikes although he really *seemed* entitled to two or three balls.

That is a fatal mistake. Two wrongs do not make a right. And you may have won and lost the game with your second and consciously wrong decision, whereas your first wrong one, which was a genuine error, may have done no harm at all. Thus, the third man at the bat, he whom you called out on strikes which were not all strikes, might have been able to hit a home run on the fourth ball pitched—but you never let him get that fourth ball. Had the second man at bat—him you gave an unearned base on balls—been properly called out, that home run, which is always a possibility, might have won the game. Whereas with the third man out, the batter who wrongfully got to first base not only had no chance to score, but gave an additional chance to put out the man at bat, who, if he knocked a grounder, could either be retired himself, or be put out by the side being put out, the man on first being retired at second on a force play.

To repeat, therefore—two wrongs don't make a right, and the tendency to "be fair" by giving one side an advantage, unearned, because you have just handicapped the other side with a decision you realize later was wrong, can never be considered good umpiring.

As an umpire, you will find that the game looks very different either from behind the rubber, or from within the diamond, from the way it looks when you are playing. You will also realize that the difference between a ball and a strike is one of a fraction of an inch sometimes and very difficult to determine. Yet you *must* call either a ball or a strike, and make your decision instantly and stick to it—otherwise the whole game will become chaotic and nobody will be satisfied. You will find that with a runner on the bases your troubles multiply greatly, and you will have the opportunity to learn how it feels to try to look three ways at once. When umpiring from behind the pitcher, you must watch him to see that he makes no balk; watch the batter to see that he is in his box and not crowding the plate illegally; watch the coachers to see that they do not step where they do not belong; watch the base-runner to see when he starts to steal or where he is when the ball is thrown to first in an endeavor to catch him napping; watch, at the same time, a base-runner on his bag and an outfielder making a catch; and first of all, you must watch the ball and see where it goes, and whether it crosses the plate or not, and, if so, whether it is high or low.

Many an umpire takes his eye off the ball the instant the runner starts to steal second, and turns and watches the flying figure. But a single umpire cannot afford to do this, and if you will watch a big League umpire who is so unfortunate as to have to run his game alone (almost invariably the league games now have two umpires, one behind the plate, the other on bases) you will see that his head never moves when the man starts to steal until the ball has passed the plate, and he has called "strike" or "ball" as the case may be. Then, and not till then, does he turn his head to see the runner nearing second base and whether the ball thrown by the catcher beats him to the bag or not.

The ball or strike decision on the runner's steal is just as important as any other ball or strike decision—to fail to get it and have to guess at it is bad umpiring. Moreover, there is plenty of time to watch for the ball crossing the plate and then to turn toward second base, since the runner cannot possibly be thrown out at second until the ball gets there!

You will find that, while new to umpiring, you will often make an error of judgment, and look for the play at the wrong place. An umpire has only two eyes, it is true, but he must use those two as if he had a hundred. It does not follow because there is a man on first that the play of the batted ball will be made at second, you know—you must be alert for the fielder's choice and see to it that your eyes are where the ball is, for where the ball is, there the play is, and where the play is, is where your decision is needed. Of course, this does not mean that you must look nowhere else. An excited or dishonest first baseman might even hold the belt of the runner trying to make second, when the play is being made at third, if he is sure the umpires are both watching third base. But to win the game by such tactics is not square, straight base-ball—is not base-ball at all. It is to be hoped that the lads for whom you umpire don't play that sort of game, but if any unfair trick should be used, it is your business to see it, even while you are watching the play. It is for lack of sufficiently good eyesight, for lack of quickness of decision and ability to see all that goes on, that big League umpires are so hard to get. Hundreds of ball players, experts at the game in their day, try umpiring when forced to leave the playing field from physical disability; but where a hundred try, one succeeds in demonstrating his fitness for the place.

The bad habit of calling a play before it happens is one that even some big League umpires occasionally indulge in, but it is a very bad habit and is the one cause which will make a fair minded umpire reverse his decision. For instance, the batter sends a ground ball to the short-stop, who makes a throw which will obviously beat the runner to first by several feet. The umpire, sure of his judgment of the time of arrival of the runner and of the ball, waves his arm over his shoulder signifying "out." But at that precise moment the first baseman sneezes, the ball bounds from his glove, and though he picks it up again immediately, the runner has crossed the bag. The umpire, seeing a dropped ball, has to reserve his decision, and stand with both hands in front of him, palms down, indicating "safe." The play was called before it happened, and it didn't happen as it looked as if it was surely going to happen!

If this should chance to be the third play of the inning, such a decision might well have a marked effect in the scoring. Thus, if it was the third out and the man really *was* out, there would be no sense in the man on third base trying to score. He might see the umpire wave the runner out and turn to the player's bench without stepping on the plate. The umpire, bound to reverse his decision the moment he saw the dropped ball, would thus virtually trap the man coming in from third, who might thus be unable either to get home or get back to third. By far the best way is never to call a play until it is finished, but then to call it instantly, as you see it, and stick to it.

The lad who umpires must make up his mind to two things beforehand: One—that he will have in his mind no interest in the game, no care as to which team wins, no secret hope for one nine above the other—for in no other way can he be a just umpire. The other—that he will remember that a little "kicking" from players lets off steam and does no harm. Because a pitcher really believes a certain delivery to be a strike when you know it is a ball, is no reason for you to resent his saying so; and because a runner, called out in a close play at the plate, indignantly says "he never even touched me with the ball 'til I was over the plate" is no reason for you to think that he is insulting you even though you know that he, the runner, slid *around* the plate and not over it.

Jack Sheridan, for long the dean of the American League Umpires and now Chief of the Umpire Staff of that organization, says: "Many an umpire makes no end of trouble for himself for the reason that he does not know how to handle players. It does not do to notice everything a player says or does. I find it does no harm at all to let him do a little fretting and fuming; I pretend not to hear it at all or I simply stand and smile at the player. In most cases he will see that he is acting foolishly and go back to his position. It does not pay to bandy words, for one will lead to another and the umpire must always get the small end of it, from a home crowd. Sometimes if a player seems very hurt and feels that he is really getting the worst of it, I tell him just how and why I made the decision and that seems to have a salutary effect."

The power given umpires in the big Leagues should find some substitute in all amateur games, whether they be amateur league games, or just games "for fun." In the big Leagues an umpire, displeased with the conduct of a player, may rule him off the field, fine him money or have him suspended from play for various periods—the president of the league usually inflicting the more severe penalties on recommendations of his umpires after the player has been sent from the field for misbehavior.

In the heat of contest and particularly when you are sure the umpire has made a mistake, you are very apt to protest indignantly, and even, perhaps, to carry that protest to the point of stopping the game. It isn't really sportsmanlike, but boys sometimes let their feeling of injustice at a decision run away with them. Then, if the umpire

World's Champions, 1910 and 1911
The Athletics at Shibe Park, Philadelphia

has no real control, he must either reverse his decision to the ruination of the game, or stick to his guns and see a long wrangle followed by hot tempers and a good game spoiled.

An instance of the kind came to the author's notice recently, which is so pat, and so amusing in itself, that it cannot well be omitted. As these are real amateur teams with real young men as players and as the umpire in the case is flitting in and out of the room in which this is being written, fictitious names had best be given.

The team from Sandmouth, then, had come over, fifteen miles, to play the team of Yarwichport. It was a game for the fun of the thing only, no admission being charged. A collection taken up during the game to which each spectator contributed what pleased him, was used entirely to defray the expenses of traveling, the balls, the diamond, etc.

The umpire was the superintendent of a large summer home estate in Yarwichport—a first class umpire is William, too, who sings out his decision on the instant and sticks to it! He has studied the rules, too, and even though his own son pitched for Yarwichport, no one, least of all no member of the visiting team, doubted either his ability or his honesty.

The visiting team had been brought the fifteen miles from Sandmouth in two big automobiles, owned by the man for whom William works—a summer resident of Yarwichport, and much interested in all sports and in the local amateur team.

In the first half of the ninth, with one out, a man on first and the score two to two, the Yarwichport pitcher hit the batter on the hand with a pitched ball. The Sandmouth contingent let out a yell of delight, and were immensely incensed that the umpire refused to allow the struck batsman to take his base, or the man on first to go to second. An immediate wrangle ensued, in which *all* players of both sides except the man on first, the pitcher and the second baseman of the nine in the field, took part. The umpire "flocked by himself" to use his own expression and wouldn't even listen to the discussion. Voices were getting angry and tempers rising when the captain of the Sandmouth nine announced that he would stop playing then and there, if that decision wasn't reversed.

Whereupon the summer resident who had brought the players over from their home fifteen miles distant strode into the group and delivered himself as follows: "I don't know anything about the facts in this case—I only saw what you all saw, and there seems to be a difference of opinion as to the facts. But I do know that you boys agreed to come over here and play a game of ball, that you agreed heartily on William as an umpire and agreed to play under him and abide by his decisions. Now if you think he is unfair, or partial or ignorant, you don't have to play under him—another time. But this time you have agreed to play under him, agreed to abide by his decisions, and you must abide by your word. I agreed to bring you over here in my machines and to take you home again when the game is ended. You break your word and refuse to play this game out, and, so far as I am concerned, you will walk home."

The game was finished and Yarwichport won, three to two.

As a matter of fact, the umpire was right, since the man at bat had made no effort to avoid the ball. But even if he had made every effort to avoid the ball, and the umpire hadn't seen it, or chose to have the man stay at the plate, that was the umpire's business. Such summary methods of compelling obedience to an umpire as were used in this case are not always available, but it makes a much better game, if both sides post a forfeit—say of half a dozen balls, or a few bats, or the like, that both will obey the umpire—and post those forfeits in the hands of some older person, who will see that they are properly returned or forfeited as the agreement is or is not lived up to.

There is one other way—it is by far the nicer way, if you can manage it—and that is, for every lad on both teams to agree "honor bright" to abide by the decisions of the umpire, and make it a point of honor not to protest decisions of fact. In the old days, the player who "kicked" at a decision was called "baby" because he could not "take his medicine." If you will just consider for a moment that protesting an umpire's decisions of fact—whether you are "out," or "safe," or whether it was a "ball" or a "strike," is merely an attempt to get something for yourself to which you are not entitled, you will readily see that such kicking has no rightful place in the game. A tennis player who kicks at an umpire's decision is considered hardly a gentleman. Englishmen would scorn to kick at the decisions of the umpire in cricket, and we know the English to be the nation which has fathered athletic sports for years.

Learn to hold your tongue and your temper in leash. Play with another and a better umpire next time, but make it a matter of personal pride to uphold *this* umpire *this* time, even if it costs you the game.

Modern base-ball, greatest of games, is a business. All amateur play is modeled on the games, the rules, the actions of leagues and players in organized base-ball. A National Commission decides what the rules shall be, and officiates, *through the umpires* in the several leagues, at all the games, and settles disputes.

Because base-ball is a professional sport, a game played for gain, by players who make the playing a business, it has been found necessary in leagues to depart from the old ideas of fair play as a guide, and conduct all games strictly in accord with rules and laws, previously agreed upon by players, teams, and leagues. The immediate result has been to pave the way for a contest within a contest. Ball teams strive against each other for scores, and even against rules and umpires, to get, when possible, an advantage which the rules do not permit.

Here is the broad divisional line between the professional and the amateur players. Few boys expect to be professional players when they grow up—every boy wants to be as good a player as his favorite model. The lad who has charge of second base for his nine worships the name of Lajoie of Cleveland, Evers of Chicago, Collins of Philadelphia,—the short-stop cannot read enough about Hans Wagner the Great, of Pittsburgh—outfielders look upon the swift and daring Tyrus Cobb of the Detroit Tigers as the greatest man in the game. To the young pitcher, Mathewson, Brown, Plank, Walsh, are names to conjure with—young wearers of the mit wonder at the speed and accuracy of second base throws as delivered by an Archer, a Gibson, a Bresnahan or a Street.

To imitate men like these in the actual playing of the game is a worthy ambition. These players are at the top of their profession because they are the best—the swiftest, the strongest, the most accurate. But no boy can afford to imitate the professional ball player in the contest of wits which goes on between him and the umpires. It is not considered a violation of honor or of ethics for a base-runner to "cut a base" in a professional game, *if he can do it without the umpire seeing him.* To do this on purpose in an amateur game, governed possibly by only one, and perhaps anything but an expert, umpire, is, and should be, an unpardonable offense on a nine playing for love of the game.

Underlying all American sports is the idea of fair play. The boy who cheats at marbles is ostracized at school quite as quickly as he who "cribs" his Latin in the classroom. Fighting with fists, temper all gone and only a savage desire to "beat him up" left, no healthy American boy would strike below the belt, or hit his opponent when he is down. Two boys cannot set upon one in any American school yard. Fair play is a trait of character which begins in the kindergarten.

A rule and penalty covering every conceivable violation of a rule has been made a part of the game. A recent instance in a big League game, with names omitted for obvious reasons, shows the reason and the necessity. There were two out, a man on third, and two strikes called. The batter hit a high foul which went close to the grandstand. The catcher, mask on the ground, ran for the ball. He was running hard, with his face upturned, his eyes on the falling ball. The manager of the team with a man at bat rose from his chair, caught it by the handle and thrust it at the inrunning catcher, jerking it back and sitting on it again, all in an instant. The catcher, seeing something from the corner of his eye, and fearing he knew not what, stopped short, the ball fell to the ground, and the batsman, of course, was not out. The umpire, however, was watching the play, saw the interference, and promptly called the man at bat and the side, out, on account of the interference.

Here was a case where a bit of foul play was covered by the rule. Yet if the umpire had not actually seen the interference, no matter if a thousand people told him it had occurred, he could not have remedied the violation of the rule which allows a man to complete a play without interference from any one. The offending manager took a chance that the umpire wouldn't see him. Actually, he did his side more harm than good, for the catcher might have missed the foul anyway. As it was, *he*, if not the ball, was caught, and his side lost its chance to score represented by the man on third.

There is a classic instance of a base-runner, who, in the old single-umpire days started to run from first base on a ball hit down the right foul line. The right fielder, playing deep, could get the ball only on the bound. He threw to the plate, trying to get a runner. The umpire was giving all his attention to this close play. The man who started from first, seeing this, cut second base by forty feet, running almost straight across the diamond from first to third. Of course, the crowd went crazy and there was a near-riot, but the umpire, having only one pair of eyes and those busy elsewhere, didn't *see* this gross violation of the rules and had to allow the runner to stay on third, from which position he subsequently scored!

It was base-ball, under the rules, but it wasn't honest playing. With many professional players the motto sometimes seems to be "Win the game if you can by playing fair—but win the game!"

With the amateur it should be, always, "Win the game by playing fair—or lose it!"

For every new trick to beat the rules, there is a new rule and penalty. The player who tries to avoid the rules, takes a chance, the penalty for getting caught at which is usually an out, or an involuntary assist of the opposing side. The man who cuts a base may be put out by fielding the ball to that base. The man who interferes with another player makes it possible for that player to make his base without more effort than is required to walk—for the umpire gives it to him! The pitcher who tries to catch a base runner with a false motion of his arm, commits a balk, and the player gets his base!

The professional player who is tricky is not to be considered dishonest or accused of unfair play, because what he does is a part of the professional game, and is so understood.

But the amateur, admiringly imitating the professional, should stop at that point. To play fair, to win only by playing the better game, is a foundation not only for character, but for success in sport in later years, and for the liking and respect of one's fellow players and fellow men.

But right here comes a very fine, almost invisible, line, marking a very delicate distinction, yet one which is an actuality and which must be recognized. There is a difference between playing unfair ball, and playing ball to avoid some of the rules. It is almost impossible to put in words as an abstraction, yet an example will make it clear. The batter hits and runs for first base. Short-stop scoops up the ball and throws wild to first base. First baseman gets in the runner's way, catches the ball, both are thrown to the ground, first baseman beats runner to the bag in the scramble—batter out.

Has the first baseman played unfairly in getting in the runner's way? Certainly not.

But suppose the ball is thrown straight for the baseman. The pitcher runs diagonally across the path of the runner, just in front of him. He is going to back up the first baseman in case the ball is wide. He manages so the runner just doesn't collide with him, but does have to shorten his stride. Is the pitcher unfair in what he has done? According to the strict logic of the intent of the rules he is—according to base-ball and the way it is played, he isn't.

Yet if the pitcher had held out his arm and touched the runner or held him, the rules would call the runner safe for interference.

Custom makes certain technical violations of the rules right—and because there cannot be laws to provide for these violations—or perhaps, because umpires are but human and can neither see all these little violations or look into a player's mind and know that he has made an unfair play, they have grown to be a part of the game. Base-runners in college, amateur and professional teams alike, will start from one base for another before a fly ball is caught—just a little before, but still, *before*. The umpire cannot watch right field and third base at once, nor tell which happened first, the ball dropping in the glove or the foot leaving the bag. "Beating the catch" is considered fair, even though against the rules, simply and because it is a small technical violation which cannot usually be detected. Every good pitcher has a good "balk" motion—that is, he makes runners think he is going to throw to base when he is going to pitch. "Balking" is against the rules and a penalty is provided for it, yet there is an invisible, intangible, impossible-to-name balk which every good pitcher has, or tries to get, to "hold 'em on the base" or "catch 'em going back"—and it is part of the game.

Fielders are not supposed to block runners off the bases—that is, they are not supposed to deliberately get in the runner's way and keep him from touching the bag while they, the fielders, catch the ball and touch the runner. That is a matter of rule. But what umpire is going to be able to tell the difference between an intentional block and one made because the fielder could stand nowhere else when he caught the ball thrown to him? So blocking off the base, and more particularly blocking off at the plate, are well recognized incidents of the game.

When a man hits a home run which isn't "over the fence," did you ever notice all the basemen standing on their bags? That is to make the runner run as far outside the bags as possible—and lose time. Did you ever notice the short-stop get in the runner's way and make him swerve a little, and then suddenly start for the plate to "back up the catcher," crossing the line in front of the runner, actually making him slow up just a little? It is a well known trick and if artistically done it is considered fair by players and allowed by umpires.

Signal stealing, if done by eyes and wits, as already referred to, is certainly a legitimate part of the game—but even the professional frowns on the semaphore and the electrical attachment to help his side get the other side's signals.

On the other hand, the doctoring of playing grounds is certainly unfair, even though to some extent the practice is general in professional ball. The rules provide absolutely the size, shape and condition of the playing field—to raise the pitcher's box to help a tall pitcher get a "down cross fire" delivery—to flatten the pitcher's box out until it is below the level of the infield to help an undersized pitcher deliver "sky rockets," to bank the foul lines to keep the bunts of a bunting team from going foul, to alter the level of the bases or the distance between them, is entirely and emphatically unfair.

"How, then, shall we know," you may ask, "which rule violation is 'fair' and which is 'unsportsmanlike.'" And it is a difficult question to answer in one sentence. But try this for a guide—"Breaking a non-enforceable rule, when the other side can see, understand, and do the same" is not unsportsmanlike. "Breaking the enforceable rule and daring the penalty, in the hope that the umpire won't see it, is not sportsmanlike."

That permits blocking at the plate, crossing in front of the runner and sliding to first base, but prohibits cutting a base, altering grounds or deliberately interfering by touch or thrown object, with the runner. And the distinction, which will seem fine drawn to the theorist, is practical and will be understood by all boys who play, and want to play, fair.

There is no end to base-ball, and since each pennant race brings out new stars, new plays, new tricks and plans, so base-ball is always new, always to be written about, always to be enjoyed afresh, by the spectator who has seen his thousand games as well as by the lad playing his first "real game."

But no papers on the subject, written with whatever expert knowledge, no books treating of the game, written with whatever enthusiasm for the green diamond, the white ball, the dusty uniform and the dear sound of ball against bat, can make a player of the reader.

You have found out, long ago, that, given a ball hit four feet to the right of the first baseman, the runner is out, if you field it, the pitcher covers first, and you make a good toss, unless the umpire calls him safe! You have had, probably many times, sharp lessons that base-ball advice is of more interest than real use, since it is the unexpected which happens on the ball-field; the boy who "never hits" may suddenly poke out a home run when you least expect it, and the sure double play sometimes ends in disaster because the ball "wouldn't go straight." But you must also have learned that although base-ball luck is a potent factor in the game, real skill and brains win here, as elsewhere, in the long run, especially if aided by good batting! You have learned that there is no royal road to stardom on the ball-field or on any other field, but that earnest practice and much thinking will improve any one's play, and time and hard trying will make a good player out of almost any one able to run and catch a ball.

While you who play base-ball now, as boys cannot all grow up to be Cobbs, Lajoies, Collinses, Wagners, Everses, Mathewsons, Bakers, Walter Johnsons, or Hal Chases, you can remember that what once has been done can always be done again; that no play on the ball-field is beyond your reach simply because you are not known to fame as a ball-player. And, last of all, you can remember, and remember well, that the greatest of all players has to yield obedience to his manager or field captain, as the greatest of all soldiers must to his "general orders." Of all the many fine things in a game of base-ball—and they *are* many—there is none finer, even as there is nothing grander in warfare, than the self-sacrifice of the individual for the good of the many, the playing for the team and for the game and for the win, instead of for the wild applause for individual acts, and the resulting merely temporary fame.

If in any way this book has helped you to win, or to make a losing game a close one, if within these pages you have found even a few hints which will enable you to organize a better team, to work, as a team, more as big League teams work together,—in other words, to play a better game of base-ball,—the time and effort spent in writing it will have been well spent, and the writer will be glad of the opportunity he has had to talk to the American boy about the grand American game.

How I Became a Big-League Pitcher

BY CHRISTY MATHEWSON

Few of the boys who read this article will become big-League pitchers. The majority of them probably have no such ambition. But nearly all boys play ball, and almost all boy players wish, at some time, to be pitchers.

The first necessity for a pitcher is to have control of the ball. That can't be emphasized too strongly. A boy may be able to throw all the curves imaginable, but if he can't put the ball where he wants it, the batters keep walking around the bases, and he will never win any ball games. Therefore, I would, first of all, advise my young readers to practise accuracy, until they can place the ball just where they want to send it. Let them pitch to another boy, with a barn or a fence as a back-stop, and try to put one *high*, over the *inside* of the plate, the next *low* over the inside, and then high over the *out*side, and again low over the outside; and keep up this practice patiently until mastery of the control of the ball is obtained. A boy will find that even if he can't pitch a curve, but has good control, he will be able to win many more ball games than if he has a lot of benders, but no ability to put the ball where he wants it.

There used to be a pitcher in the American League, named "Al" Orth, who was called the "Curveless Wonder," because, it was said, he couldn't throw a curve ball. But he had almost perfect control, and was able to pitch the ball exactly where he thought it would be hardest for the batter to hit it. The result was that, for several years, he was one of the best pitchers in the American League, with nothing but his control to fall back upon. But he studied the weaknesses of batters carefully—that is, he was constantly on the alert to discover what sort of a ball each batter couldn't hit—and then he pitched in this "groove," as it is called in base-ball.

When I was a boy about eight or nine years old, I lived in Factoryville, Pennsylvania, a little country town; and I had a cousin, older than I, who was always studying the theory of throwing. I used to throw flat stones with him, and he would show me (I suppose almost every boy knows) that if a flat stone is started with the flat surface parallel to the ground, it will always turn over before it lands. That is, after it loses its speed, and the air-cushion fails to support it, the stone will turn over and drop down. The harder it is thrown, the longer the air sustains it, and the farther it will carry before it drops.

My cousin showed me, also, that, if the hand were turned over, and the flat stone started with the flat surface at an acute angle to the earth, instead of parallel to it, the stone, instead of dropping, would curve horizontally. I began to practise this throw, and to make all sorts of experiments with stones.

I got to be a great stone thrower, and this practice increased my throwing power, and taught me something about curves. When I was nine years old, I could throw a stone farther than any of the boys who were my chums. Then I used to go out in the woods and throw at squirrels and blackbirds, and even sparrows; and many a bag full of game I got with stones. But, when aiming at game, I always used round stones, as these can be thrown more accurately.

All this time I was practising with stones, mainly for amusement; I hadn't played any base-ball, except "one old cat," with boys of my own age. As a matter of fact I didn't think much about base-ball. Gradually, however, I became interested in it, and before long, I was allowed to stand behind the catcher when the Factoryville team was playing, and "shag" foul balls, or carry the bats or the water. For I was born with the base-ball instinct, and a "mascot," or bat-boy, is the role in which many a ball-player has made his start.

This Factoryville nine was composed of grown men, and it was not uncommon for small town teams to wear whiskers in those days. Many of the players, too, were really fat men. But, boy-like, I felt very important in being "connected with" this pretentious-looking club. My official name was "second catcher," which entitled me to no place in the batting order, but gave me a chance at all foul balls and other misplaced hits that none of the regular nine could reach. If I happened to catch a wild foul ball, I would often hear the spectators say, "That's a pretty good kid. He'll make a ball-player some day." But if I missed one, then it would be: "That kid's pretty bad. He'll never be a ball-player!"

So, at the age of ten, I became a known factor in the base-ball circles of Factoryville, and might be said to have started on my career.

My next step was learning to throw a curve with a base-ball, and one of the pitchers on the town team undertook to show me how this was done. He taught me to hold the ball for an outcurve, and then to snap my wrist to attain the desired result. After considerable practice, I managed to curve the ball, but I never knew where it was going. I used to get another youngster, a little younger than I, up against a barn, with a big glove, and pitch to him for hours. At last, I attained fair control over this curve, and then I began practising what is known in the big Leagues as the "fast ball," but what most boys call an "in-curve."

Every boy knows that, if he grips a ball tightly and then throws it, with all his speed, off the ends of his fingers, the ball will curve in toward a right-handed batter slightly. This curve is easy to accomplish, as it is merely a matter of speed and letting the ball slide straight off the ends of the fingers,—the most natural way to throw. It does not require any snap of the wrist, but the bend of the curve is naturally slight, and that is the reason most big Leaguers call it a fast ball, and do not recognize it as a curve. At the age of twelve, having no designs on the big League, I called it the "in-curve," and reckoned, with some pride, that I could throw two curves,—the "out" and the "in."

I first began playing ball on a team when I was twelve, but most of the other boys were older than I, and, as pitcher was considered to be the most important position, one of the older boys always took the job without even giving me a tryout. In fact, they thought that I was altogether too good a pitcher for my age, because I had considerable speed, and it was natural that several of the older boys didn't want to see the "kid" get along too fast. So they put me in right field, on the theory that "*anybody* can play right field."

I wasn't much of a ball-player, outside of being a pitcher, and it must be confessed that I never showed up brilliantly with that boy team. I could catch flies only fairly well, could throw hard and straight, and was pretty good at chasing the balls that got away from me; but I wasn't a good hitter, and probably for just one reason.

I was what is known as a "cross-handed" batter,—and the experts will all tell you that this is a cardinal sin in a batsman. It means that I stood up to the plate as a right-handed batter does, but put my left hand on top of my right, which greatly reduces the chances of hitting the ball when a man swings at it. All boys should be careful to avoid this cross-handed method of holding the bat. It is a great weakness. No one that I played with knew enough to tell me to turn around and bat left-handed, or that I was probably, by nature, a left-handed hitter. I would advise any boys who have this fault to try hitting left-handed, and if this does not prove successful, to practise keeping the right hand on top until they are able to swing that way. No one will ever be a good ball-player who hits in the clumsy, cross-handed style.

I believe I got the habit from hoeing, and chopping wood, and performing some of the other chores that a country boy is called upon to do. At all events, it "came natural," as the saying is, for me to hold my left hand on top of my right when doing any work of that kind. The result was, that I batted as if I were hoeing potatoes, and seldom obtained a hit. Once in a while, I would connect with the ball, in my awkward, cross-handed style, and it would always be a long wallop, because I was a big, husky, country boy; but more often I ignominiously struck out. So it will be seen that my real base-ball start was not very auspicious.

But, even then, I would rather play base-ball than eat, and that is the spirit all boys need who expect to be good players. When I was fourteen years old, the pitcher on the Factoryville team was taken ill one day, just before a game with a nine from a town ten miles away, and the contest was regarded as of great importance in both villages. Our second pitcher was away on a visit, and so Factoryville was "up against it" for a twirler. You must remember that all the players on this team were grown men—several of them, as I have said, with whiskers on their faces, and roly-poly bodies—but I had always looked up to them as idols. When the team could find no pitcher, some one remarked to the captain: "That Mathewson kid can pitch pretty well." But the backers of the team and the other players were skeptical, and, like men who come from Missouri, "wanted to be shown." So they told me to come down on the main street in Factoryville the next morning, which was Saturday, the day of the game—and take a "tryout."

"We want to see what you've got," said the captain to me.

Most of the base-ball population of the town gathered to see me get my tryout, and I pitched for two hours, while the critics stood around and watched me closely, to discover what I could do. They sent their best batters up to face the curves I was throwing, and I was "putting everything that I had on the ball." After a full hour's dress rehearsal, and when, at last, I "fanned" out the captain of the team, he came up, slapped me on the back, and said:

"You'll do. We want you to pitch this afternoon."

That, I am sure, was the very proudest day of my life. We had to drive ten miles to the opponent's town, and all the other boys watched me leave with the men. And you can imagine my pride while *I* watched *them*, as they stood on one foot and then the other, nudging one another and saying, "'Husk' is going to play with the men!" They called me "Husk" in those days.

It was a big jump upward for me, and I would hardly look at the other youngsters as I climbed into the carriage with the captain. If the full truth were told, however, I felt almost "all in" after the hard session I had been through in the morning.

I can remember the score of that game yet, probably because it was such an important event in my life. Our team gained the victory by the count of 19 to 17—and largely by a bit of good luck that befell me. With my hands awkwardly crossed on the bat, as usual, I just happened to swing where the ball was coming *once*, when the bases were full, and I knocked it over the left-fielder's head. That lucky hit won the game; and that was really my start in base-ball.

This happened toward the end of the summer season; and in the fall I went to the Keystone Academy, after having completed the public-school course, there being no high school in Factoryville at that time.

I played on the Keystone team during my first year at the academy, but I was still young, and they thought that it was up to some older boy to pitch, so I covered second base. I was playing ball with boys sixteen, seventeen, and eighteen years old at this time, and I was only fourteen.

The next year, however, I was captain of the team, and pitched (the natural result of being elected captain, as any of my readers know who may have led base-ball clubs!). While I was the captain of this team, I hit upon a brilliant idea, which really wasn't original, but which the other boys believed to be, and so it amounted to the same thing. When we were playing a weak team, I put some one else into the box to pitch, and covered second base myself, to "strengthen the infield." We had a couple of boys on the team who—like certain twirlers in every league—could pitch, but couldn't bat or play any other position. I caught this idea from reading an article in a newspaper about McGraw and the Baltimore "Orioles." I worshiped him in those days, little thinking that I should ever know him; and it was beyond my fondest dreams that I should ever play ball for him.

I was still batting cross-handed on the Keystone team; but, in pitching, I had good control over my out-curve which was effective against the other boys. During the vacation of that summer, I pitched for the Factoryville team, until it disbanded in August, which left me no place to play ball, and, remember, at that time I still would rather play ball than eat, and, big, growing boy that I was, I was decidedly fond of eating!

But one fine day, the captain of a team belonging to a town about five miles away came to me and asked if I would pitch for his nine.

"We'll give you a dollar a game!" he said in conclusion.

"What! How much?" I asked, in amazement, because it as such fun for me to play ball, then, that the idea of being *paid* for it struck me as "finding money."

"A dollar a game," he repeated; "but you'll have to walk over, or catch a ride on some wagon."

There was no trolley route connecting the two villages then. I told him he needn't mind how I got there, but that I would certainly come.

So, for a time, I went regularly over to the other town—Factoryville's old rival—and pitched every Saturday; and often I had to walk both ways. But they always gave me my dollar, which was a satisfactory consolation and a good antidote for foot-weariness. By this time, I was far ahead of boys of my own age, in pitching, and was "showing them how to pitch," and rather regarding them as my inferiors, as any boy will, after he has played with men.

In 1898, I was graduated from Keystone Academy, and as I had played foot-ball there, and was a big, husky, country kid, I was regarded as a desirable student by several colleges, and urged by friends at the University of Pennsylvania and by others at Lafayette College to enter one of those institutions of learning. But I finally decided to go to Bucknell.

During that summer, I happened to be in Scranton, Pennsylvania, soon after school closed. It looked a big city to me then, and the buildings seemed to be very high. As I was only there for the day, I made up my mind that I would make sure of seeing the Y.M.C.A. team play ball, which it did every Saturday. At the hour appointed for the game, I was sitting in the grand stand munching peanuts, when it was suddenly discovered that the Y.M.C.A. pitcher was missing, and they began to look around for some one to twirl.

One of their players, it seems, had seen me pitch in Factoryville, and, having recognized me in the stand, he went up to the captain of the team, and said: "There's a kid up there who can pitch."

"Where's he from?" asked the captain.

"Factoryville," replied my friend.

"I don't think he'll do," said the captain. "Those small-town pitchers don't make good when they stack up against real ball teams. But I'll remember him, and I may have to try him if the regular pitcher doesn't show up."

The regular pitcher didn't "show up," and the result was that the two players came over to me, some ten minutes later, where I was still munching peanuts in eager anticipation of the game, and began a conversation in this wise:

"Can you pitch?" the captain asked me.

"A little," I replied.

"Want to work for us this afternoon?"

I was startled. Then, "Sure I do!" I exclaimed, and promptly climbed down over the front of the stand, leaving quite three cents' worth of peanuts on the seat, which was no compliment to my natural country thrift, and indicated that I was excited. They handed me a uniform, very much too big for me, the one that the regular pitcher usually wore, and as I was putting it on in the dressing-room, I began to wonder if the job would be as much too large. When I came out and the crowd got a look at me, everybody began to ask who the big country boy was with the misfit uniform.

But I "had something" that day, and struck out fifteen men.

"You're a pitcher!" said the captain to me after the game, and he ordered a uniform made to fit me. I was seventeen at that time, and was still playing with teams whose members were all much older than I. And that was the second opportunity to pitch that came to me through a "break in the luck," as ball-players say.

At midsummer of that year, I went to Honesdale, Pennsylvania, where I was given twenty dollars a month and my board, to pitch for the team there. This seemed to me then a princely salary, and I began to speak of "J. P. Morgan and me."

In 1898, I matriculated at Bucknell, and played foot-ball there. This is a college of less than two hundred male students, but the class of men was generally high. The next summer I went back to Honesdale, after having played on the Bucknell base-ball team. And, in the middle of the season, I was offered ninety dollars a month to pitch in the New England League, a salary which turned out to be only on paper, for the Taunton club disbanded before I was ever paid, and I received only an occasional five or ten dollars, which promptly went to the landlady.

Honesdale proved to be an important mile-post in my base-ball journey. Two things I learned during my stay there, and both have been of great value to me. First, and most momentous, I discovered the rudiments of "the fade-away"; and, second, I stopped batting cross-handed. This correction of my hitting style was the result of ridicule. I was very large by this time—almost as big as I am now—and when I came up to the bat, with the wrong hand on top, and swung at the ball, I looked awkward. The players on the other teams, and the spectators began to laugh at me and "guy" me. "Look at that big boob trying to hit the ball!" they would shout as I missed one.

I made up my mind to change my style, and I started to try to hit with the right hand on top, standing up to the plate right-handed. It was very hard for me at first, and for a long time I couldn't hit nearly as well that way as I could with my hands crossed; but I stuck to the new style, knowing that it would be a big improvement in the end. I had batted the other way so long that it was hard for me to correct it. That is the reason I advise all boys with a tendency to hold a bat with the wrong hand on top to change *immediately*, because the longer they keep on hitting in that way, the harder it will be for them to adopt a new style. No one will ever be a hitter, swinging in

Mathewson Pitching a Fast One
Copyright by Paul Thompson

this awkward manner, because the hands cannot guide the bat accurately. Since I changed my batting form, I have developed into a fair-hitting pitcher.

In Honesdale, there was a left-handed pitcher named Williams who could throw an out-curve to a right-handed batter. Now the natural curve for a left-handed pitcher is the in-curve to a right-handed batter, and Williams simply exhibited this curve as a sort of "freak" delivery, in practice, over which he had no control. He showed the ball to me, and told me how he threw it, and I began to wonder why a right-handed pitcher couldn't master this delivery, thus getting an in-curve to a right-handed batter on a slow ball, which surely seemed desirable. Williams pitched this ball with the same motion that he used in throwing his in-curve, but turned his hand over and snapped his wrist as he let the ball go. He could never tell where it was going to break, and therefore it was of no use to him in a game. He once played a few games in one of the big Leagues, but lasted only a short time. He didn't have enough control over this freak ball to make it deceptive, and, as far as the rest of his curves were concerned, he was only a mediocre pitcher.

But it was here that I learned the rudiments of the fade-away, and I began to practise them with great diligence, recognizing the value of the curve. I also started to pitch drop balls while I was in Honesdale, and mixed these up with my fast one and the "old roundhouse curve." I only used the drop when the situation was serious, as that was my very best, and a surprise for all the batters. Few pitchers in that set, indeed, had a drop ball.

The part of the summer with the Taunton team apparently did me little good, beyond teaching me the style of base-ball played in the New England League, and proving to me that there is sometimes a great difference between the salary named in a contract and that received. As a matter of fact, however, that portion of a season spent in the New England League was going to have a great influence on my future, although I could not foresee it at the time.

I returned to Bucknell in the fall, where I played full-back on the foot-ball team; and, oddly enough, I was much better known as a foot-ball player at this time than as an exponent of base-ball. Probably this was because I developed some ability as a drop-kicker, and, at college, foot-ball was considered decidedly the more important sport. Moreover, I received poor support on the college base-ball team; and no pitcher can win games when his men don't field well behind him, and thus lose the game for him, or when they refuse to bat in any runs.

In the fall of 1899, the Bucknell foot-ball team went down to Philadelphia to play the University of Pennsylvania eleven, and this proved to be one of the most important trips that I ever took. While our players were waiting around the hotel in the morning, a man named John Smith, known in base-ball circles as "Phenom John" Smith, came around to see me. He was an old pitcher, and had picked up the name of "Phenomenal (shortened to "Phenom") John" in his palmy days in the box. He had been the manager of the Portland club in the New England League during the previous season, and had seen me pitch with the Taunton nine.

"Mathewson," he said to me, "I'm going to Norfolk in the Virginia League, to manage the club next season, and I'll give you a steady job at eighty dollars a month. I know that your contract called for ninety dollars last season, but you will surely get this money, as the club has substantial backing."

I signed the contract then and there. The colleges weren't as strict about their men playing summer ball at that time. *Now* I would advise a boy who has exceptional ability as a ball-player, to sign no contracts, and to take no money for playing, *until* he has finished college. Then, if he cares to go into professional base-ball, all right.

"I'm going out to see you play foot-ball this afternoon," said Smith, as he put the contract in his pocket.

I was lucky that day, and kicked two field goals against Pennsylvania, which was considered to be a great showing for a team from a small college, in an early season game, regarded almost as a practice contest. Field goals counted more then—five points each—and there were few men in the country who were good drop-kickers.

Hudson, the Carlisle Indian, was about the only other of my time. Those two field goals helped to temper our defeat, and we lost by about 20 to 10, I think. When I got back to the hotel, "Phenom John" was there again.

"You played a great game this afternoon," he said to me, "and, because I liked the way in which you kicked those two field goals, I'm going to make your salary ninety dollars instead of eighty dollars."

He took the contract, already signed, out of his pocket, and raised my pay ten dollars a month before I had ever pitched a ball for him! That contract is framed in Norfolk now, or rather it *was* when I last visited the city with "the Giants" on a spring-training trip. The old figures remain, with the erasure of the eighty and the correction of ninety just as "Phenom John" made them with his fountain-pen.

As you will easily believe, I went back to Bucknell very much pleased with myself, with two field goals to my credit in foot-ball, and in my pocket a contract to play base-ball for ninety dollars a month.

The rest of the story, until I got into the big League, is brief.

I went to Norfolk the next summer, and won twenty-one games, out of twenty-three, for the team. And on a certain day in the midsummer of 1900, "Phenom John" Smith came up to me, smiling in the friendliest way.

"Matty," he began, "I've never regretted changing that contract after it was signed. You have played good ball for me, and now I have a chance to sell you to either the New York National League club or the Philadelphia club. Which team would you rather be with?"

This came to me as a great surprise, the opportunity to "break into the big League"—the dream of my life. Only one year before, I had stood outside the player's gate at the Polo Grounds, on my way to Taunton, and had lingered to watch Amos Rusie, the great pitcher of the Giants, make his exit, so that I could see what he looked like in his street clothes, and also contribute a little hero-worship in the way of cheers. Now I was going to be member of a big-League club myself!

"I'll let you know in a couple of days," I told Smith, in reply to his question about my choice of the two clubs.

Then I began to study the list of pitchers with each team. The Giants were a vastly different organization then from that of today, and were usually found near the bottom of the list toward the end of the season. But they were *in need* of pitchers, and so I decided that, if I went with New York, I, a youngster, would have a better chance to pitch regularly. They hadn't much to lose by making a thorough trial of me, and they might give me an opportunity to work, was the way I reasoned it out.

"I'd like to go to New York," I told Smith; and, needless to say, I have never regretted my decision.

That is how I became a big League pitcher, in the middle of the summer of 1900, at the age of nineteen years. George Davis was the manager of the New York club at the time, and the first thing he did when I reported for duty was to summon me for morning practice.

"Now," he said, "I'm going to order all our fellows to go up to the bat, and I want you to throw everything you've got."

He started off himself, and I was nervous enough, facing the manager of a big-League team for my tryout. I shot over my fast one first, and I had a lot of speed in those days.

"That's a pretty good fast ball you've got, there," declared Davis. "Now let's have a look at your curve."

I threw him the "old roundhouse" out-curve, my pride and joy which, as the newspapers said, had been "standing them on their heads" in the minor league. He stepped up into it, and drove the ball over the head of the man playing center field and beyond the old ropes.

So was an idol shattered, and my favorite curve wrecked!

"No," he said, "that 'old roundhouse' curve ain't any good in this company. You can see that start to break, all the way from the pitcher's box. A man with paralysis in both arms could get himself set in time to hit that one. Haven't you got a drop ball?"

"Yes," I answered; "but I don't use it much."

"Well, let's have a look at it."

I threw him my drop ball, and he said that it was a pretty fair curve.

"Now that's what we call a curve ball in the big League," declared Davis. "As for that other big one you just threw me,—forget it! Got anything else?"

"I've a sort of a freak ball that I never use in a game," I replied, brimful of ambition.

"Well, let's see it."

Then I threw him my fade-away, although it hadn't been named at the time. He missed it by more than a foot (I was lucky enough to get it over the plate!). I shall never forget how Davis's eyes bulged!

"What's *that* ball?" he asked.

"That's one I picked up, but never use," I answered. "It's a kind of a freak ball."

"Can you control it?"

"Not very well."

"Try it again!" he ordered. I did, and got it over the plate once more. He missed the ball.

"That's a *good* one! That's all right!" he declared enthusiastically. "It's a slow in-curve to a right-handed batter. A change of pace with a curve ball. A regular fall-away or fade-away. That's a good ball!"

And there, in morning practice, at the Polo Grounds in 1900, the "fade-away" was born, and christened by George Davis. He called some left-handers to bat against it. Nearly all of them missed it, and were loud in their praise of the ball.

"Now," said Davis, in the club-house after the practice, "I'm not going to pitch you much, and I want you to practise on that fade-away ball of yours, and get so that you can control it. It's going to be a valuable curve."

So every morning I was out at the grounds, trying my fade-away, and always aiming to get control of it—absolute, sure precision. I worked hours at a time on it, and then Davis would try me out against batters to see how it was coming along. He didn't give me a chance in a regular game until toward the end of the season, when he put me into a contest that had already been lost by some other pitcher who had been taken out.

But, the next spring, just before the opening game of the season of 1901, Davis came to me and said:

"Matty, I want you to pitch tomorrow."

This command was a big and sudden surprise to me. I went home and to bed about nine o'clock, so as to be feeling primed for the important contest. And the next day it rained! Again I went to bed early, and once more it rained! I kept on going to bed early for three or four nights, and the rain continued for as many days. But I finally outlasted the rain, and pitched the opening game, and won it. Then I worked along regularly in my turn, and didn't lose a game until Memorial Day. And that brought me up to be a regular big-League pitcher.

Many persons have asked me how I throw the fade-away. The explanation is simple: when the out-curve is thrown, the ball is allowed to slip off the end of the thumb with a spinning motion that causes it to bend away from a right-handed batter. The hand is held up. Now, if the wrist were turned over and the hand held down, so that the ball would slip off the thumb with a twisting motion, but, because the wrist was reversed, would leave the hand with the thumb toward the body instead of away from it, I figured that an in-curve to right-handed batters would result. That is how the fade-away is pitched. The hand is turned over until the palm is toward the ground instead of toward the sky, as when the out-curve is thrown, and the ball is permitted to twist off the thumb with a peculiar snap of the wrist. The ball is gripped in the same way as for an out-curve.

Two things make it a difficult ball to pitch, and the two things, likewise, make it hard to hit. First of all, the hand is turned in an unnatural position to control, or throw, a ball when the palm is toward the ground. Try to throw a ball with the hand held this way, and you will find it very difficult. Next, that peculiar snap to the wrist must be attained. The wrist is snapped away from the body instead of toward it, as in the throwing of an out-curve, and it is an unnatural motion to make. The secret of the curve really lies in this snap of the wrist.

Many times I have tried to teach other pitchers in the big League—even men on opposing clubs,—how to throw this ball, but none have ever mastered it. Ames, of the Giants, can get it once in a while, and Drucke oftener, but it is a ball which requires a great deal of practice. It is a hard ball to control, and unlimited patience must be used. If any boy desires to try it, let them practise for control first, and then try to make the curve bigger. Be sure to turn the hand over with the palm toward the ground, and throw the ball by snapping the wrist away from his body, which will send it spinning slowly up to the batter. It comes up "dead," and then drops and curves in.

In conclusion, as at the beginning, I want to emphasize the value of control for young pitchers. Let a boy practise control, always, before he starts to learn curves; for again let me assure him that he will win many more games if he can throw the ball where he wants to and hasn't a curve, than if he has a big curve but can't control the ball. Another thing that a young pitcher must be careful about is the way in which he holds the ball. When I went to Norfolk to pitch, I was wrapping my fingers around the ball when I was going to throw a curve, so that it was evident to the batter what was coming. "Phenom John" Smith came to me one day and said: "Matty, you'll have to cut that out. You telegraph to the batter by the way in which you wrap your fingers around the ball every time you are going to throw a curve. It won't do in this League."

I began to practise holding the ball in the same way for each kind of delivery, and then adjusting my fingers as I made the motion to let the ball go from my hand. Boys should practise this,

Mathewson at the Finish of the Famous Fade-Away
Photo by Paul Thompson

also, as it is fatal to wrap the fingers around the ball in such a way that a batter can see when a curve is coming. A pitcher should cover the ball up with his glove when facing the batter, anyhow.

I always hold the ball in the same way for every curve, that is, with my whole hand around it, and not with two or three fingers wrapped on it. For a change of pace, I hold it loosely so that the ball can be thrown with the same motion as for a fast one. Sometimes, for a drop, I hold my fingers on the seam, in order to get more purchase on the ball.

Many persons have asked me about the "moist," or "spit" ball. I seldom use it, because I think it is hard on a pitcher's arm, and difficult for the catcher to handle and for the players to field. It has many disadvantages. Occasionally, I used to try one on "Hans" Wagner, the great batter of the Pittsburgh club, because it was generally believed that he didn't care for a moist ball, but this, too, is only one of the many "theories" of base-ball. He can hit a moist ball as well as any other kind! and I have stopped pitching it altogether, now.

The only reason that I ever used it was to "mix 'em up." Next to control, that is the whole secret of big-League pitching—"mixing 'em up." It means inducing a batter to believe that another kind of a ball is coming from the one that is really to be delivered, and thus preventing him from "getting set" to hit it. That is what gives the fade-away its value. I pitch it with the same motion as a fast ball, but it comes up to the plate slowly. The result is that the batter is led to believe a fast one is coming, and sets himself to swing at a speedy shoot. The slow ball floats up, drops, and he has finished his swing before it gets to the plate. I often pitch the fade-away right after a fast ball; and, as for reports that I can't control it, I use it right along when I have three balls and two strikes on a batter, which is the tightest situation a pitcher has to face. For it is a ball that will usually be hit slowly, on the ground to the infielders, if the batter hits it at all. Its value, as I have said, lies in the surprise that it brings to a batter when he is expecting something else.

I have often been asked, if it is such a difficult ball to hit, why I don't use it all the time. The answer is that such a course would make it easy to bat, and, besides, it is a ball which strains and tires the arm.

Finally, I want to say that "Phenom John" Smith did a great deal toward developing me as a pitcher. He pointed out my weaknesses as he saw them, and gave me a great deal of valuable advice. If any of my readers expect to play big-League ball, let them find some friendly "Phenom John" Smith and get his advice. There are scores of old ball-players, ever ready to help an ambitious youngster, and they are the best-natured men in the world. And once more: remember that *control* is the thing in pitching! No man was ever a big Leaguer for long without it.

THE END

A. G. Spalding's Simplified Rules

The Ball Ground

Base-Ball is played upon a level field, upon which is outlined a square, which is known as the infield or "diamond." The term "diamond," in a broader sense, is also frequently used in the United States to apply to the entire playing field. Literally, however, the "diamond" is the infield proper.

The infield is bounded by the base-running paths, which extend from base to base. The bases are placed at right angles to each other, on each corner of the "diamond," at intervals of ninety feet beginning from the home plate. Thus first base must be ninety feet from home plate, second base ninety feet from first base, third base ninety feet from second base and also ninety feet from the home plate, thus completing a perfect square.

The territory which lies behind third base, second base and first base, beyond the infield and within the lines defining fair ground and also without these lines, is known as the outfield. All that portion of the field outside of the base lines that extend from home plate to first base and from home plate to third base, all territory behind the home plate and all territory outside of straight lines reaching from the outside corner of third and first bases indefinitely to the outfield is foul ground.

Sometimes it is impossible for boys who desire to play baseball to obtain a field sufficiently large for the regulation diamond, whose dimensions have previously been stated, and in such cases an effort should always be made to place the bases at equal distances from each other in order that the symmetry of the diamond and the correct theory of the game may be preserved. *Players of younger years may find that a smaller diamond adds more enjoyment to their amusement, since they are better able to cover the ground in fielding the ball in a smaller area and do not become so fatigued by running the bases when the latter are stationed at their full legal distance from each other.*—(Italics are the author's.)

The bases, except home plate, are best constructed of canvas bags filled with sawdust. Home plate should be of whitened rubber, whenever it is possible to obtain it. Some cruder substance may be used for bases if nothing else is obtainable, but it is best to follow the suggestions given. First, second and third bases should be attached to pegs driven in the ground, and home plate should be sunk so that its upper surface is on a level with the surface of the ground.

The pitcher's position on a diamond of regulation size is located sixty and five-tenths feet from home plate, and on a straight line, extending from home plate to the center of second base. It, too, should be denoted by a plate of whitened rubber, to be sunk until its upper surface is on a level with surface of the field. This plate should be the shape of a parallelogram twenty-four inches long by six inches wide, with the longer sides of the parallelogram at right angles to home plate.

If a diamond smaller than the regulation size be used, the pitcher's position should be relatively closer to home plate.

The Ball.

The Spalding Official National League Ball is used in regulation games, but for players fifteen years of age or younger, the Spalding Official "National League Junior" ball, made the same as the National League Ball, only slightly smaller in size, should be used, for it better fits the boy's hand and prevents straining the arm in throwing.—(Italics are the author's.)

The Regulation Bat.

The bat must always be round and not to exceed 2¾ inches in diameter at the thickest part.

Regulation Gloves and Mitts.

The catcher or first baseman may wear a glove or mitt of any size, shape or weight. Every other player is restricted to the use of a glove or mitt weighing not over ten ounces and measuring not over fourteen inches around the palm.

Players' Uniforms.

Games played by players not clad in a regular uniform are called "scrub" games and are not recorded as "match" games. Every club should adopt a regular uniform, not only to enable the players to play properly and with comfort, but to distinguish one team from the other.

Player's Benches.

All ball grounds should be provided with two players' benches of and on each side of the home plate. They must be not less than twenty-five feet outside of the coacher's line. The coachers may not go within fifteen feet of the base lines. Each team should occupy one of these benches exclusively, and their bats and accoutrements should be kept near the bench.

Field Rules.

No person shall be allowed upon any part of the playing field except players in uniform, the manager of each side (and the latter not when the game is in progress, except that he is in uniform); the umpire and the officers of the law. No manager, captain, or player is supposed to address the spectators. In a regular League match this is considered a violation of the rules.

Soiling and Providing Balls.

No player shall be allowed to soil a new ball prior to putting it into play.

In League games the home team provides the ball. It is customary in smaller leagues to expect the home team to do the same. The umpire has the custody of the ball when it is not in play, but at the conclusion of the game the ball becomes the property of the winning team.

Number and Position of Players.

Two teams make up each contest with nine players on each side. The fielders are known as the pitcher, the catcher, the first baseman, the second baseman, the third baseman, the short-stop, the left fielder the center fielder and the right fielder. None of these is required to occupy an exact position on the field, except the pitcher, who must stand with his foot touching the pitcher's plate when in the act of delivering the ball to the batter, and the catcher, who must be within the "catcher's space" behind the batter and within ten feet of home plate. Players in uniform must not occupy seats in the stands or mingle with the spectators.

Substitute Players.

It is always advisable to have a sufficient number of substitutes in uniform ready to take the field in case any player shall become disabled or be disqualified.

It is the duty of the captain of each team immediately to announce changes of players to the umpire, and the umpire shall announce them to the opposing team and spectators.

When a pitcher is taken from his position his substitute must continue to pitch until the batsman has reached first base or has been put out.

Choice of Innings—Fitness of Field for Play.

The home team has the choice of innings and determines whether the ground is fit for play providing it has rained before the beginning of the game. If two clubs from the same city are playing, the captain of the team on whose ground the game is played has the choice of innings.

A Regulation Game.

The game begins with the fielders of the team losing the choice of innings in their respective positions. The first batter of the opposing team is in his "box" at home plate. This "box" is a parallelogram, six feet by four, on either side of home plate, and six inches back from the furthest corner of the plate.

If it is not possible to outline a "box" it should be remembered that the batter is never allowed to step over home plate to strike at the ball, and that he must not run forward toward the pitcher, to exceed three feet from the center of the plate, to strike at the ball.

The umpire may take his position, at his option, either behind the pitcher or the catcher. He judges all balls and strikes, declares all outs, decides whether the ball is batted foul or fair, decides as to the legality of the pitcher's delivery, and, in fact, has complete control of the game. His decisions must never be questioned, except by the captain of either team, and only by the latter when there is a difference of opinion as to the correct interpretation of the rules.

The team at bat is allowed two coaches on the field, one opposite first base and the other opposite third base, but they must never approach either base to a distance closer than fifteen feet, and must not coach when there are no runners on the bases.

Whenever a player is substituted on a nine he must always bat in the order of the man who retires from the game. A player may be substituted at any time, but the player whose place he takes is no longer eligible to take part in the contest.

When a substitute takes the pitcher's place in the box he must remain there until they batsman then at bat either is retired or reaches first base.

A game is won when the side first at bat scores fewer runs in nine innings than the side second at bat. This rule applies to games of fewer innings. Thus, whenever the side second at bat has scored more runs in half an inning les of play than the side first at bat it is the winner of the game, provided that the side first at bat has completed five full innings as batsmen. A game is also won, if the side last at bat scores the winning run before the third hand is out.

In case of a tie game play continues until at the end of even innings one side has scored more runs than the other, provided that if the side last at bat scores the winning run before the third hand is out the game shall terminate. This latter provision applies to a regular nine-inning game. Rulings relative to drawn games and games that are called because of atmospheric disturbances, fire or panic will be found under the head of "Umpire's Duties."

PITCHING RULES.

Before pitching the ball the pitcher must face the batsman with both feet squarely on the ground and in front of the pitcher's plate. When the ball is delivered the pitcher must face the batter and one of his feet must be in contact with the pitcher's plate. Not more than one step must be taken in the act of delivery.

Whenever the ball after being pitched and without striking the ground goes over any part of home plate between the knee and the shoulder of the batsman it must be called a strike, whether the batsman strikes at it or not.

If the pitcher fails to deliver the ball over any part of the plate, or if he delivers it over the plate above the shoulder or below the knee and the batsman declines to strike at it, it is called a ball, or if the bases are unoccupied, any ball delivered by the pitcher while either foot is not in contact with the pitcher's plate shall be called a ball.

If the ball touches the ground before it passes home plate and is not struck at by the batsman, it is a ball and must be called as such by the umpire. If struck at, it is, of course, recorded as a strike.

At the beginning of each inning the pitcher is allowed to throw five balls to the catcher or to an infielder for "warming-up" practice, the batsman refraining from occupying his position in the "box" at home plate.

After the batsman steps into his position the pitcher must not throw the ball around the infield, except to retire a base-runner. If he violates this rule and, in the opinion of the umpire, is trying to delay the game, the umpire may call a ball for every throw thus made. If the pitcher occupies more than twenty seconds in delivering the ball to the batter the umpire may call a ball for each offense of this nature.

The pitcher must not make any motion to deliver the ball to the batsman and fail to do so, nor must he feint to throw to first base when it is occupied by a runner and fail to complete the throw. Violation of this rule constitutes a balk which gives all runners who are on the bases at the time an opportunity to advance a base without being put out.

A balk is also declared when the pitcher throws to any base to catch a runner without stepping directly toward that base in the act of making the throws; when either foot of the pitcher is behind the pitcher's plate when he delivers the ball; when he fails to face the batsman in the act of delivering the ball; when neither foot of the pitcher is in contact with the pitcher's plate in the act of delivering the ball; when, in the opinion of the umpire the pitcher is purposely delaying the game; when he stands in his position and makes any motion with any part of his body corresponding to his customary motion when pitching and fails immediately to deliver the ball; when he delivers the ball to the catcher when the latter is outside of the catcher's box.

When a pitched ball, at which the batsman has not struck, hits the batsman before the catcher touches it, the umpire must call it a dead ball and no base-runner can advance. The batsman, however, must be in his position at the time that the ball hits him and must make every effort to get out of the way of the ball if he fears that it will hit him.

If a batsman makes a foul strike, if a foul hit is not caught, if the umpire declares a dead ball, or if a fair hit ball touches a base-runner or umpire, if the pitcher makes a balk, or if there is interference with fielder or batsman, the ball is not in play until after it has been returned to the pitcher, standing in his position, and the umpire has given the word to resume play. No base-runners may advance when the ball is not in play.

Whenever a person not engaged in the game touches a batted or thrown ball, a block follows. This must at once be announced by the umpire, and runners shall be privileged to advance bases until the ball is thrown to the pitcher, standing in his position. After that they advance at their peril. The pitcher may then throw a runner out wherever he sees a possibility of doing so. Should a spectator retain possession of a blocked ball, or throw it or kick it out of the reach of the fielder who is endeavoring to recover it, the umpire must call "Time," and hold all runners at such bases as they occupied when he called "Time" until after he has permitted play to resume, with the ball returned to the pitcher standing in his position.

Batting Rules.

Before the game begins each captain must present the batting order of his team to the umpire, who shall submit it to the captain of the other side. This batting order is followed throughout the game except when a player is substituted for another, the substitute batting in the order of the retired player.

Each player of each nine must go to bat in his regular order unless a substitute has been authorized to take his place.

After the first inning the first batter in each succeeding inning is the player following the man who completed his full time at bat in the inning before. For instance, if a batter has but one strike in the first inning and the third hand be put out while he is at bat, he becomes the first batter in the following inning, not having completed his full time at bat in the inning previous. In such case, any balls and strikes called in the previous inning do not count when he resumes his time at bat.

Players of the side at bat must remain on their seats on the player's bench except when called upon to bat, to coach, or to act as substitute base-runners.

No player of the side at bat except the batsman is privileged to stand in the space behind the catcher, or to cross it while the pitcher and catcher are handling the ball.

Players sitting on the bench of the side at bat must get out of the way of fielders who approach them while trying to field a batted or thrown ball.

Any legally batted ball that settles on fair ground (the infield) between home and first base, or between home and third base, or that bounds from fair ground to the outfield inside of first base, or third base, or that touches the person of a player or the umpire on fair ground, is a fair hit.

A fair hit is also any legally batted ball that first falls on fair territory beyond first base or third base.

Any legally batted ball that settles on foul ground is a foul hit, except that a ground hit, should it roll from foul to fair territory between first and home and third and home, and remain there, is a fair hit.

A ground hit that first strikes fair territory and rolls outside of the foul line between first and home, or third and home, is a foul hit.

Any legally batted ball that falls on foul territory beyond first base, or third base, or that touches the person of a player or an umpire on foul ground, is a foul hit.

A foul tip is the continuation of a strike which has merely been touched by the bat, shoots directly into the hands of the catcher and is held by him.

A bunt hit is legally tapping the ball slowly within the infield by the batsman. If a foul result, which is not legally caught, the batsman is charged with a strike, whether it be the first, second or third strike.

Any hit going outside the ground is fair or foul as the umpire judges its flight at the point at which it passes beyond the limitations of the enclosure in which the contest takes place. A legal home run over a wall or a fence can only be made when the wall or fence is 235 feet from the home plate. This rule is not invariably followed in amateur games.

If the batsman strikes at a pitched ball and misses it, a strike is called.

If the batsman fails to strike at a pitched ball which passes over the plate at the proper height, a strike is called.

A foul tip caught by the catcher is a strike.

A foul hit, whether a fly or a ground hit, bounding to any part of foul ground, is a strike unless the batter has two strikes. After two strikes the batter may foul the ball without penalty unless he bunts or is caught out on a foul fly.

All bunts rolling foul are strikes. If the batsman strikes at the ball and misses it, but the ball hits him, it is a strike.

If the batsman, with either of his feet out of the batsman's box, hits the ball in any way it is a foul strike and the batsman is out.

If a batsman bats out of turn and it is discovered after he has completed his time at bat, but before the ball has been delivered to the succeeding batsman, the player who should have batted is out, and no runs can be scored, or bases be run, on any play made by the wrong batter. This penalty is not enforced unless the error has been discovered before the ball is delivered by the pitcher to the succeeding batsman.

If the error is discovered while the wrong batsman is at bat, the proper player may take his place, but he must be charged with whatever balls and strikes have already been recorded against the wrong batsman. Whenever this happens the batters continue to follow each other in their regular order.

Should the batsman who is declared out for batting out of order be the third hand out, the proper batsman in the next inning is the player who would have come to bat had the side been retired by ordinary play in the preceding inning.

The batsman is out if he fails to take his position within one minute after the umpire has called for him.

The batsman is out if a foul fly, other than a foul tip, is caught by a fielder, providing the latter does not use his cap, his protector, or any illegal contrivance to catch the ball, and providing the ball does not strike some object other than a fielder before being caught. It has been ruled that when the ball lodges in the catcher's protector by accident and he secures it before it falls to the ground, the catch is fair. This is a very exceptional play.

The batsman is out whenever he attempts to hinder the catcher from fielding or throwing the ball, either by stepping outside of the lines of his position or by deliberate obstruction.

The batsman is out when three strikes are called and first base is occupied, whether the catcher holds the ball or not, except there be two hands out at the time.

The batsman is out, if, while attempting a third strike, the ball touches any part of his person, and base-runners are not allowed to advance.

Before two men are out, if the batsman pops up a fly to the infield with first and second, or first, second and third bases occupied, he is out if the umpire decides that it is an infield hit. The umpire shall immediately declare when the ball is hit whether it is an infield hit or an outfield hit. It is customary for the umpire to call the batter out in case that he decides it an infield hit, so that base-runners may be protected and not force each other out through the medium of a double play.

The batsman is out on a bunt that rolls foul if the attempted bunt be made on the third strike.

The batsman is out if he steps from one batsman's box to the other after the pitcher has taken his position to pitch.

Base-Running Rules.

After the batsman makes a fair hit in which he is not put out he must touch first, second and third bases, and then the home plate in regular succession in order to score a run.

No base-runner may score ahead of the man who precedes him in the batting order if that player is also a base-runner.

The batsman must run to first base immediately after making

a fair hit, or when four balls have been called by the umpire, or when three strikes have been declared by the umpire. If the batsman is hit by a pitched ball, either on his person or clothing, and the umpire is satisfied that the batsman did not purposely get in the way of the ball, and that he used due precaution to avoid it, he is entitled to run to first base without being put out.

The batsman is entitled to run to first base without being put out if the catcher interferes with him or tries to prevent him from striking at the ball.

The batsman is entitled to first base, without being put out, if a fair hit ball hit either the person or clothing of an umpire or a base-runner who is on fair ground.

Whenever the umpire sends the batsman to first base after four balls have been called, or for being hit by a pitched ball, or because he has been interfered with by the catcher, all runners on bases immediately ahead of him may advance a base each without being put out. A runner on second or third base with first base unoccupied would not be considered a runner immediately ahead.

Any base-runner is entitled to advance one base when the umpire calls a balk.

Any base-runner is entitled to advance one base when the ball, after being delivered by the pitcher, passes the catcher and touches any fence or building within ninety feet of the home plate. The penalty in regard to touching a fence or building is frequently waived by mutual consent where the ground area is limited.

If a fielder obstructs a base-runner the latter may go to the next base without being put out, providing the fielder did not have the ball in his hand with which to touch the runner.

All base-runners may advance three bases whenever a fielder stops or catches the ball with his cap, glove, or any part of his uniform detached from its proper place on his person.

Should a thrown or pitched ball strike the person or clothing of an umpire on foul ground, the ball is not dead, and base-runners are entitled to all the bases they can make.

The base-runner shall return to his base without liability of being put out when a foul is not legally caught, when a ground ball is batted foul, or when the batter illegally bats the ball.

On a dead ball the runner shall return to his base without liability of being put out, unless it happens to be the fourth pitched ball to the batter, in which case, if first, or first and second base, or first, second and third bases be occupied, runners shall advance to the next bases in regular order. If by accident the umpire interferes with the catcher's throw, or a thrown ball hits the umpire, on fair ground, the runner must return to his base and is not to be put out. If a pitched ball is struck at by the batsman, but missed, and the ball hits the batsman, the runner must return to his base and may not be put out. If the umpire is struck by a fair hit ball before it touches a fielder, or the umpire declares the batsman or another base-runner out for interference. In any of the above cases the runner is not required to touch any intervening bases to reach the base to which he is legally entitled.

If after the third strike has been called and missed by the catcher the then batsman attempts to hinder the catcher from fielding the ball, he is out.

Any fly ball legally hit by the batsman and legally caught on fair or foul ground is out.

Three strikes are out if the catcher holds the ball. In case he drops it, but picks it up, and touches the batsman, or throws it to first base, and the first baseman touches the base, or the batsman, before the latter can get to first base, the batsman is out.

Should the batsman make a fair hit and in the last half of the distance between home plate and first base run more than three feet outside of the base line, he is out, except that he may run outside of the line to avoid interference with a fielder trying to field the ball as batted. This rule is construed rather liberally owing to the great speed with which runners have to go to first base.

Whenever the runner is on the way from first to second base, second to third base, or third base to home plate, or in reverse order trying to secure the base which he has just left, he must keep within three feet of a direct line between bases. If he runs out of line to avoid being touched by a fielder, he is out. However, if a fielder is on the line trying to field a batted ball, the runner may run behind him to avoid interference and shall not be called out for it.

Interference with a fielder attempting to field a batted ball retires the runner, unless two fielders are after the same hit, and the runner collides with the one whom the umpire believes to have had the lesser opportunity to field the ball.

The runner is always out at any time that he may be touched by the ball in the hands of a fielder, unless the runner is on the base to which he is legally entitled. The ball, however, must be held by the fielder after he has touched the runner. If the runner deliberately knocks the ball out of the fielder's hands, to avoid being put out when not on base, he shall be declared out.

If a runner fails to get back to a base after a foul or fair hit fly ball is caught other than a foul tip, before the ball is fielded to that base and legally held, or the runner be touched by a fielder with the ball in his hands before he can get back to the base last occupied, the runner is out, except that if the ball be thrown to the pitcher, and he delivers it to the batter, this penalty does not apply. If a base should be torn from its fastenings as the runner strikes it, he cannot be put out.

If a runner is on first base, or runners are on first and second bases, or on first, second and third bases, and the ball shall be legally batted to fair ground, all base-runners are forced to run, except in the case of an infield fly (previously referred to), or a long fly to the outfield. Runners may be put out at any succeeding base if the ball is fielded there and properly held, or the runners may be touched out between bases in the proper manner. After a foul fly is caught, or after a long fly to the outfield is caught, the base-runners have the privilege of trying for the next base.

A base-runner hit by a legally batted ball in fair territory is out. In such case no base shall be run, unless necessitated by the batsman becoming a base-runner. No run shall be scored nor shall any other base-runner be put out except the one hit by the batted ball until the umpire puts the ball in play.

A runner who fails to touch each base in regular or reverse order, when a fair play is being made is out if the ball be properly held by a fielder on the base that should have been touched or the runner be touched out between bases by the ball legally held by a fielder, provided that the ball has not been delivered to the batsman in the meantime by the pitcher.

If a runner fails to return to the base that he occupied when "Time" was called after the umpire has announced "Play" he is out, provided that the pitcher has not in the meantime delivered the ball to the batsman.

The runner is out if he occupies third base with no one out or one out and the batsman interferes with a play that is being made at home plate.

The runner is out if he passes a base-runner who is caught between two bases. The moment that he passes the preceding base-runner the umpire shall declare him out.

When the batter runs to first base he may overrun that base if he at once returns and retouches it. An attempt to run to second base renders him liable to be put out.

If, while third base is occupied, the coacher at third base shall attempt to fool a fielder who is making or trying to make a play on a batted ball not caught on the fly or on a thrown ball, and thereby draws a throw to home plate, the runner on third base must be declared out.

If one or more members of the team at bat gather around a base for which a runner is trying thereby confusing the fielding side, the runner trying for the base shall be declared out.

If a runner touches home plate before another runner preceding him in the batting order, the former loses his right to third base.

Coaching Rules.

The coachers must confine themselves to legitimate directions of the base-runners only, and there must never be more than two coachers on the field, one near first base and the other near third base.

Scoring of Runs.

One run shall be scored every time that a player has made the legal circuit of the bases before three men are out, provided that a runner who reaches home on or during a play in which the third man is forced out, or the third man is put out before reaching first base, the runner shall not be entitled to score.

A player who makes a legal hit to fair territory is entitled to as many bases as he can advance without being put out. If a fielder is unable to get the ball home until the man has completed the circuit of the bases, the latter is entitled to a home run, provided the fielder has not made a misplay in handling the ball. The same rule applies to the making of a three-base hit a two-base hit, or a hit for one base, which is also known as a single.

A force-out can be made only when a base-runner legally loses the right to the base he occupies by the batsman becoming a base-runner and he is thereby obliged to advance.

Ground Rules.

Any special ground rules shall be understood by both team captains and the umpire, or umpires, in case there be two officials. The captain of the home club establishes the ground rules but if the visiting captain objects, the matter must be left to the umpire, who has final jurisdiction.

Umpire's Duties.

When there are two umpires, the umpire behind the plate is the "Umpire-in-Chief," and the umpire on the bases the "Field Umpire." The "Umpire-in-Chief" has full charge of the game, makes all decisions on balls and strikes and decides all fair and foul hits. If a ball is hit fair, with a runner on first, he must go to third to make a possible decision; with more than one base occupied, he decides whether a runner on third base leaves the base before a fly ball is caught, and if a runner is caught between third and home, with more than one base occupied, he decides on the runner nearest home plate. He, alone, can forfeit a game.

The Field Umpire makes the other decisions.

When there is but one umpire he has complete jurisdiction over everything.

The umpire has the right to call a draw game, whenever a storm interferes, if the score is equal on the last inning played. Calling a "draw game" must not be confounded with calling "time."

If the side second at bat is at bat when a storm breaks, and the game is subsequently terminated without further play, and this side has scored the same number of runs as the other side, the umpire can call the game a draw without regard to the score of the last equal inning. In other words the game is a draw just as it rests.

Under like conditions if the side second at bat has scored more runs than the side first at bat, it shall be declared the winner, all runs for both sides being counted.

A game can be forfeited by the umpire if a team refuses to take the field within five minutes after he has called "Play"; if one side refuses to play after the game has begun; if, after the umpire has suspended play, one side refuses to play after he has again called "Play"; if one side tries to delay the game; if the rules are violated after warning by the umpire; if there are not nine players on a team after one has been removed by the umpire. The umpire has the right to remove players for objecting to decisions or for behaving in an ungentlemanly manner.

Only by the consent of the captain of an opposing team may a base-runner have a player of his own side run for him.

Play may be suspended by the umpire because of rain, and if rain falls continuously for thirty minutes the umpire may terminate the game. The umpire may call "Time" for any valid reason.

Umpire's Authority.

Under no circumstances shall a captain or player dispute the accuracy of an umpire's judgment and decision on a play. If the captain thinks the umpire has erred in interpretation of the rules he may appeal to the umpire, but no other player is privileged to do so.

General Definitions.

"Play" is the order of the umpire to begin the game or to resume it after "Time" has been called.

"Time" is the order of the umpire to suspend play temporarily.

"Game" is the announcement of the umpire that the contest is terminated.

"Inning" is the time at bat of one team and is terminated when three of that team have been legally put out.

"Time at Bat" is the duration of a batter's turn against the pitcher until he becomes a base-runner in one of the ways prescribed in the previous rules. In scoring a batter is exempt from a time at bat if he is given a base on balls, if he makes a sacrifice hit, if he is hit by a pitched ball, or if he is interfered with by the catcher.

Scoring Rules.

Each side may have its own scorer and in case of disagreement the umpire shall decide, or the captain of each team may agree upon one scorer for the match.

Index

Compiled by Trey Strecker of the Bibliography Committee of the Society for American Baseball Research

Index